IT'S THE
Beano Book
2013
D1338227
13
SWIPE
BRIGHTY

THE BEANO
1938
2013
75
YEARS OF LAUGHTER!
THIS BOOK BELONGS TO:

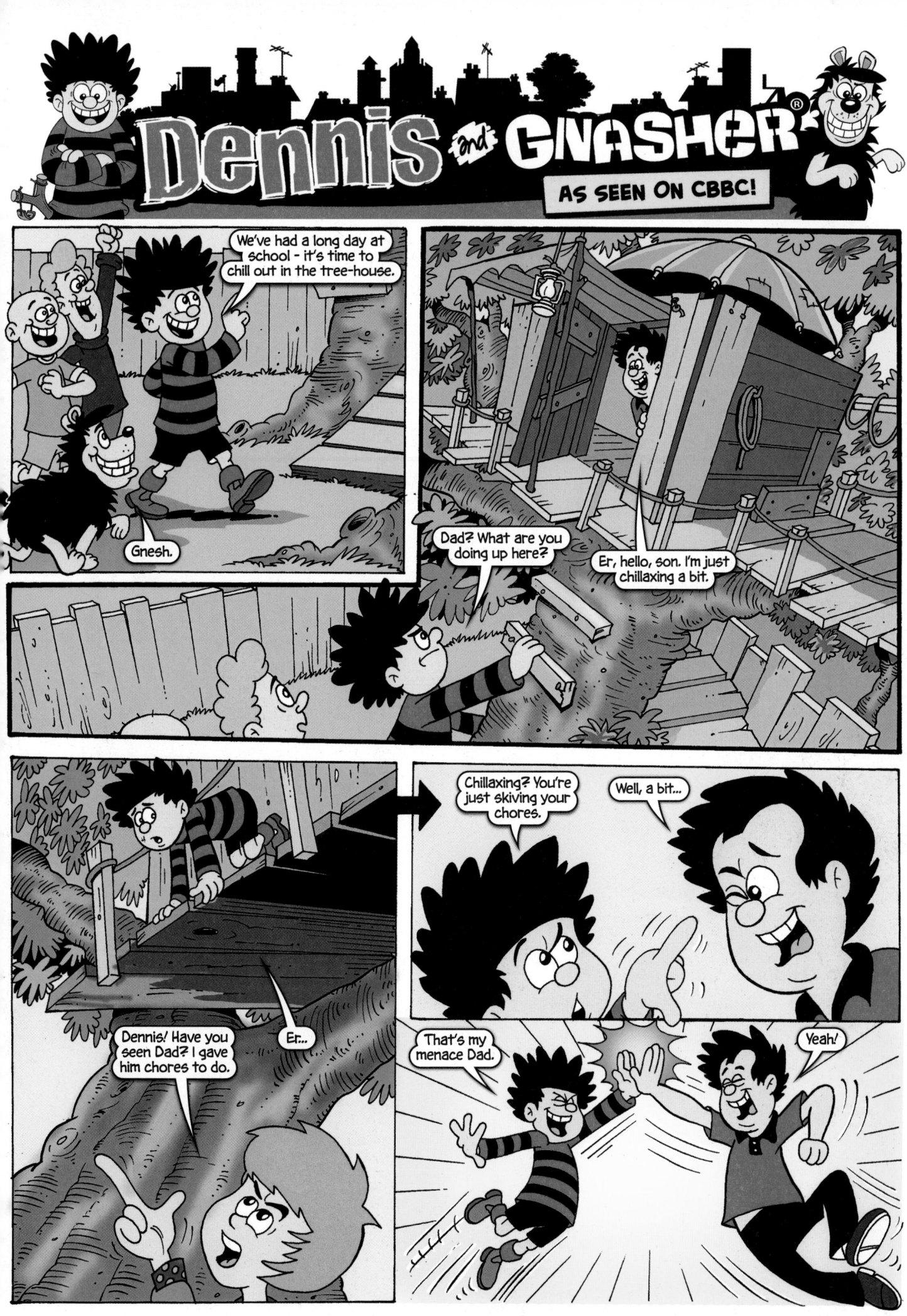
Dennis and Gnasher®
AS SEEN ON CBBC!
We've had a long day at school - it's time to chill out in the tree-house.
Gnesh.
Dad? What are you doing up here?
Er, hello, son. I'm just chillaxing a bit.
Dennis! Have you seen Dad? I gave him chores to do.
Er...
Chillaxing? You're just skiving your chores.
Well, a bit...
That's my menace Dad.
Yeah!

This is really cool! You have loads of fun and nobody can see you.
Yeah.

NEXT DAY...
Your Dad was well cool yesterday.
Yeah. He's...

...he's... here?
Hiya, Dennis. I invited some of my pals to the tree-house to skive... I mean... chill out.
My Fifth medal...
Blah-blah...
CRISPS

They've invaded our tree-house. This is really rubbish!
Tax returns...
Politics...
Boring guff...
GNASH!

NEXT DAY...
Come on, lads. We can hide out in the tree-house again.

Not today, Dads. We've taken back our tree-house. No entry to anybody over 12!
What?
Listen, Dennis. It's not nice of you not to share your tree-house. So, what do you say?
I say KNICKERS! You lot didn't share yesterday - you just invaded and took over!
SPLAT!
GMPH!
Take cover!
Heh-heh!
Lads, we can't take this lying down... CHARGE!

SLOSH!
PUFF!
SOOT
You can take our pocket-money but you'll never take our tree-house!
TWANG
WHUMP!
SOOT
SCOOSH!
OOF!
EEK!
EEPS!

Do you surrender, Dennis? I hope...
Never!
Do YOU give up?
Never ever! Nothing scares me!
SHRIEK!
Well, nothing except that shriek.
Dennis, please, help me. PLEEEEEEEASE!
Yeah, all right.
DENNIS!
Get comfy, Dad. We could be hiding up here for a while.
I think so.
Gnee-hee!
CRISPS
CRISPS
DAAAAAAAAD!
Come and tidy this mess, you two! You pair of horrors!

BALL BOY
HE'S FOOTBALL CRAZY!
Nine-nil down... and it's only half-time!
Ah... but we'll be shooting downhill second half, guys. We can still win!
It's no good - we'll never score ten to get to the cup Final!
DAVE EASTBURY
NO ENTRY
I need something to gee them up - I'll need this!
Do you know what this is? This is Mr Ned. A lucky mascot owned by my Grandad. Fourteen hours down t'pit he used to work and then play Football.
PONG!
A very old, very smelly, fluffy donkey? Poo-ee!
But I'll tell you this... this mascot helped his team - Jarrow Colliery FC - win the cup! And now it'll help you too!
Jarrow Colliery? Who are they?
Exactly, mate!
Jose Mourinho couldn't have done that better! Ho-ho!
GGRRRRRR!

AND-
See how you like playing uphill this half!
SLIDE!
Wah!

SOON-
GOAL!
I make that ten-nine to us!
BAH! GROAN!

FULL-TIME-
Woo-hoo! We've made it to the Final!
Who'da thunk it, eh? And with gravity on our side, too!
Gravity? No, we couldn't have done it without Mr Ned!
Hooray for Mr Ned!

CUP FINAL DAY-
C'mon, team! It's Cup Final day! Ninety minutes from glory!
But we're not gonna win without Mr Ned – he's our lucky mascot and he's gone missing! We'll never win without him!

But I just made that up!
Made what up, Coach?

Look – you just go out and play your normal game. I'll find Mr Ned.
Sigh. Ok, Coach. Not sure what good it'll do.

CUP FINAL
PIE SHOP
Crumbs! How will I find Mr Ned in this crowd?
WHY DON'T YOU SEE IF YOU CAN FIND MR NED? SEE IF COACH CAN FIND THE LUCKY MASCOT BEFORE THE FINAL BEGINS ON PAGE 100! BEANO ED.

MEEBO & ZUKY
It's time I broke a world record, I think.
I'm the judge around here, mate. I'll decide what's a world record and what isn't.
You?
JUDGE
I'll show him!
And away it goes!
AT THE FAR END OF THE TRACK...
Doop-de-doo...

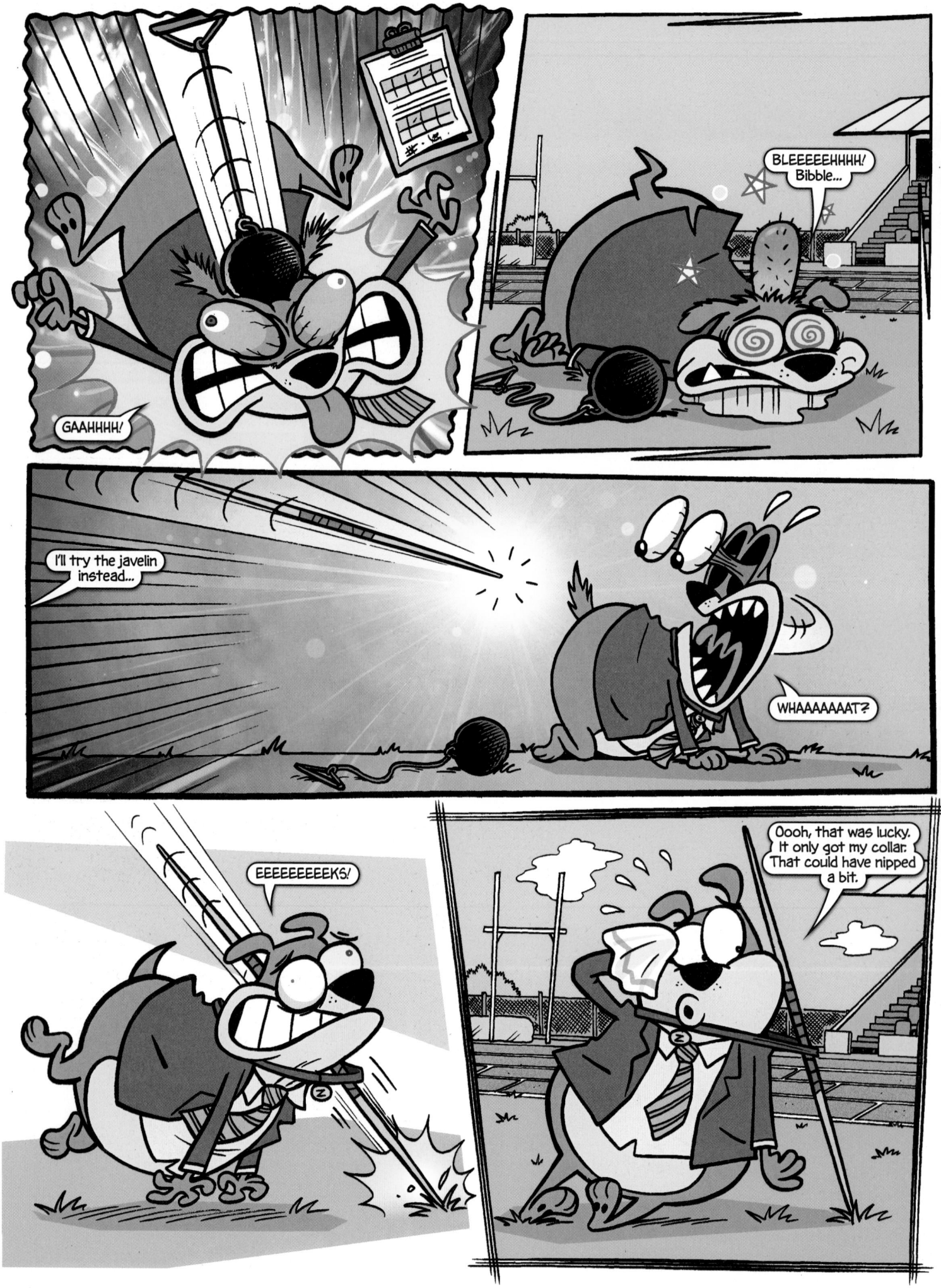
GAAHHHH!
BLEEEEEHHHH! Bibble...
I'll try the javelin instead...
WHAAAAAAAT?
EEEEEEEEEKS!
Oooh, that was lucky. It only got my collar. That could have nipped a bit.

SPINNN
HURTLE
EEEEEPS! MAD DISCUS!
YEOW!
That REALLY stings, you know - and you totally failed to break the record. Chopping off the judge's head is against the rules.
I'm not bothered...
...you can help me break the hammer-throwing world record after all. Hyuk-hyuk-hyuk!
AAAAAAAAAAAAAAAAAAAHHH!

OUR FAVOURITE PLACE
THE BASH STREET KIDS
The Sweet Factory
TOFFEE
I want a job as taster.
Om-nom-nom!
FIZZY FROTH

This is OUR favourite place in Beanotown!
These didn't have spots till I picked them up!
Candy floss
HELP!

The NUMSKULLS
This English homework is hard.
BEANO OFFICE
NUMSKULLS SCRIPT WRITER!
BRAIN DEPT.
That's why I'm helping him!
DEPT.
A tremendous essay - I'll just click 'save'...
TAP!
BRAIN DEPT.
Oh, no! I hit 'delete' by mistake!
BLANK!
?

I'm sure it won't have much effect on Edd.

Yo! 'Sup, Mo?

I was bringing you some brain food - looks like you need help with English!

And -
We need to sort this disaster!
COMMON ROOM
The BEANO ANNUAL

WE, Brainy? Seems it was your disaster!

Okay! Okay! It was my fault! As much milk and cookies as you can eat if you help me?
Barry Glennard

Milk and cookies? Why didn't you say so?
THE BEANO ANNUAL
This is what we need!
POCKET DICTIONARY
Heave!
Cut!
I'll do the first page!
50 -

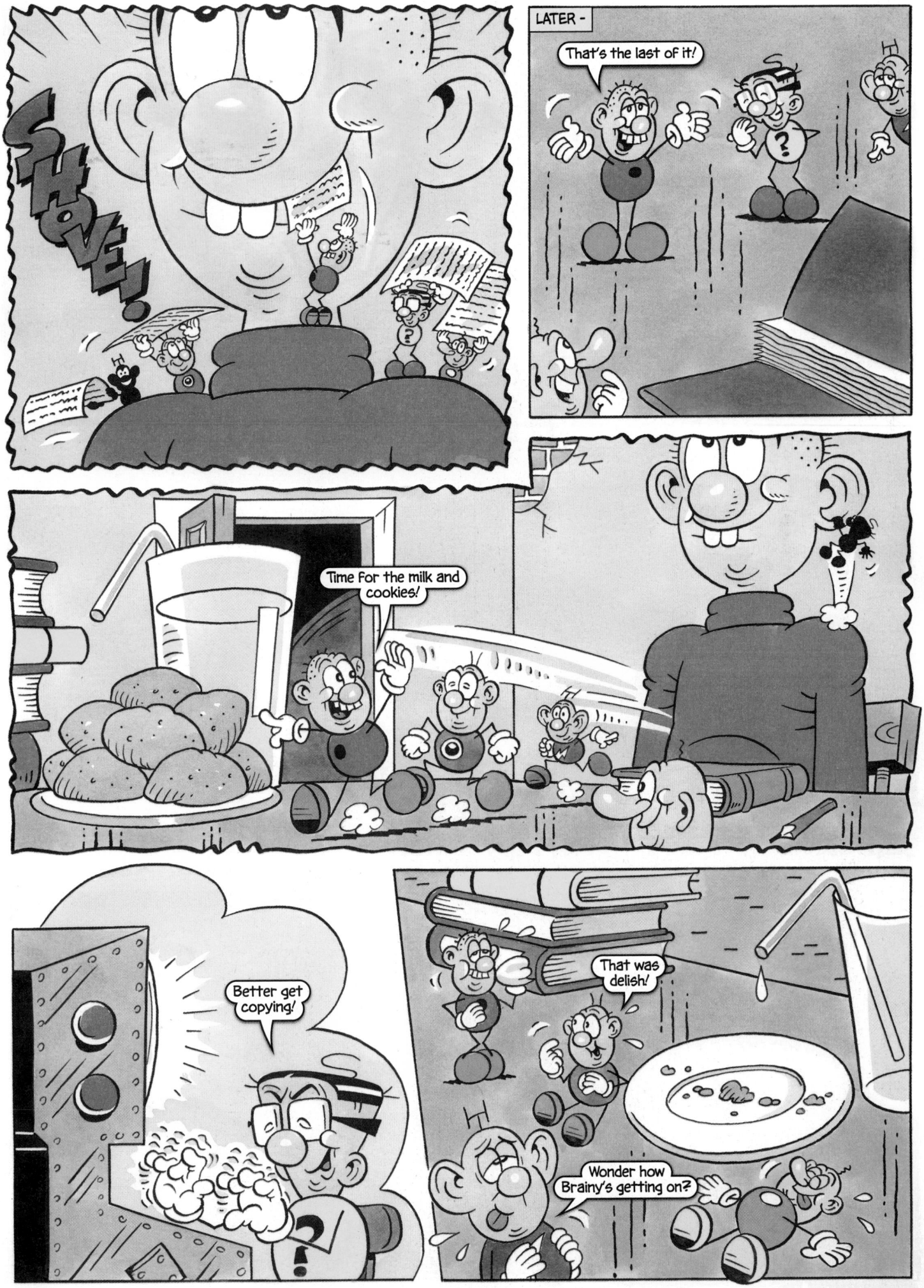
SHOVE!
LATER -
That's the last of it!
Time for the milk and cookies!
Better get copying!
That was delish!
Wonder how Brainy's getting on?

TAPPITY-TAP!
SHORTLY -
BRAIN DEPT.
Gasp! At last! Let's hope that fixes things!
Okay, son! Time for bed - that's enough studying for one night!
One can only agree with the stated hypothesis! I am ecstatically eager to perambulate upwards to alleviate my somnolent tendencies!
Huh?
Sheesh! You'd think you'd swallowed a dictionary all of a sudden!
RUFFLE!
Ha-ha! If only she knew!

GNASHER'S BITE
Snow!
Let me at it!
Er... it's deeper than I expected!
But there's fun to be had with this... just when you thought it was safe to go out in the snow...
GNASHER'S SINGING THE MUSIC FROM JAWS... IF YOU KNOW IT, JOIN IN!
...the snow-shark attacks. Da-dum... daaa-dumm...
I hate delivering parcels in the snow - but at least there's no sign of Gnasher.
AAAAAAAAGH!
GNASH!
SHARK! IN THE SNOW!
Heh-heh! The snow-shark has claimed his first victim!

BUTCHER
It's cold enough to freeze the crust off me pies!
Gnee-hee!
The snow-shark sniffs fresh meat. Gnom-nom!
I was sure I had a pile of sausages there.
I must have taken them inside... mustn't I?
And the snow-shark strikes again! Is gnobody safe?
TCHER
EEEEPS! A shark! In the snow!
BURP!
A shark in the snow? Are you sure? Right. I'm on the case!
LOST
FOUND
AND EATEN
WANTED
TOP SECRET
MIDDLE SECRET
BOTTOM SECRET

There's something fishy going on here - and I'm pretty sure it's not a shark!
That fin looks familiar... time to go fishing.
Here, fishy-fishy...
SNIFF! The snow-shark smells sausages... time to...
Got you!
...CHOMP!
OOCHA!
Gno chance! Gnothing catches the snow-shark!
I almost caught it. You should have seen this size of it. THIS big, it was...
Da-dum... Da-dum...

the BASH STREET KIDS

Bash Street's not much of a tourist destination...

CHIRP!
TWEET!
... but it does have a beauty spot!

Lovely!
BREATHE DEEPLY!

Here comes the tourist bus! Must be to see the beauty spot.
BEANOTOWN Tours
BRMM!

BEANOTOWN Tours
BRRMM
Let's wave to the nice people!

WAVE!

SWOOSH!

Fume! This means war!
WRING!

SO NEXT DAY -
Ink pellets?
CHECK LIST

Check!
TICK!
CHECK LIST
INK PELLETS
INK PELLETS

Flour bombs?
CHECK LIST

Check!

Eggs?
SIZZLE!
SIZZLE!
CHECK LIST

EGGS?
SIZZLE!
Check!

That sounds like the bus now!
PLUG'S LUG
BRMM... BRMM...

NOBODY soaks the Bash Street Kids!
BRMMM!
BEANOTOWN Tours
TOSS!
CHUCK!
HEAVE!
THROW!
TOSS!

Aiieee! Time to take evasive action!
WIPE!
SMEAR!
SPLAT!
SPLOT!
SPLAT!
WHEEE!

BEANOTOWN Tours
SWERVE!
SCREECH!
Oh-oh!

CRASH!
Phew! Everyone's all right!
BEANOTOWN Tours
That's more than can be said for the beauty spot - it's ruined!
Plug - you'll need to stand in!
Eh?

DS
FERGUSON'S FURNITURE
BEANOTOWN Tours
BEANOT Tou
We're now the only street in Britain with a genuine 'UGLY SPOT'!
Hee-hee! It's proving more popular than the beauty spot did!
SWING!
BASH STREET MUSEUM

MY FAVOURITE PLACE
DENNIS & GNASHER
Bunkerton Castle
Welcome to one's stately home!
It'll be in a real state when we're finished with it.
An old castle is great for fun!
EEKS! Scary dog!

MEEBO & ZUKY'S History of VIOLENCE
Bram Stoker's DRACULA is one of the most famous horror novels ever written.
1
Scary!
In DRACULA, an ancient vampire bites the necks of innocent people and drinks their blood.
2
Wouldn't you rather have a cup of tea?
The character of Dracula was inspired by a real prince, Vlad Dracul, who lived in 15th century Transylvania, which is now in Romania.
3
Har-har! What a stoopid hat!
Prince Vlad was better known by his nick-name... VLAD THE IMPALER.
4
I'm not sure I want to ask but... why is he called that?

YEOW! That really nips!
Vlad impaled tens of thousands of people on sharp poles.
5
Why do you think?
Some people think Vlad's use of sharp poles is why Dracula could only be killed by a wooden stake through the heart.
6
Now don't be hasty. That isn't the kind of stake I ordered.
That really stings.
THAT stings?
7
That's a rubbish book! Why don't we do Jekyll and Hyde instead?
Frankenstein is much gorier - and I can chop your head off!
And that is where we leave these two - a real pair of horrors.
8

THE GREAT ESCAPE
RATZ
Huh? Wassat? Where am I? This isn't the sewer!
I'd say not, old chap.

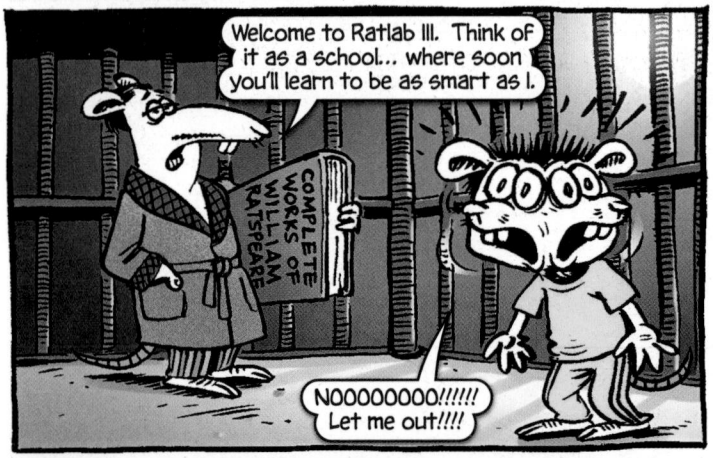
Welcome to Ratlab III. Think of it as a school... where soon you'll learn to be as smart as I.
COMPLETE WORKS OF WILLIAM RATSPEARE
NOOOOOOOO!!!!!! Let me out!!!!

Out? To some cold, dank, draughty sewer?
Hey! My sewer might be cold and dank, but it's not... what was the third one again?

I can't get through the bars 'cos they're metal. What about the floor?
The base of the cage is made from polytetrafluoroethylene. You may enjoy some small success.

Yuck! I'm not going to mention the taste as much as the poor hygiene of such an action.
GNAW GNAW

A diggin' I will go! Lend a paw, will you?
Certainly not! COUGH! You're disturbing my reading.

SOON -
This is intolerable!
No it isn't! It's just earth!

NEXT DAY-
I hope you're happy. It's taken most of the day to clean this cage.
This escape plan had better work - I've had to use the elastic from my pants!

Great cattie, this!
What do you need a cattie for, pray tell?
PLINK!

Sheesh! I thought you were supposed to be clever? To break down the door!
Oh 'eck!

SPAZ!

DONG
BING
SPANG
OOF!
Crikey!
BONG
DING

Oo – I need a lie down to recuperate!
Just borrowing your book!

NEXT MORNING-
Can I have my book back now? I'm almost finished it...
Course you can...

MADE FROM CHEWED-UP BOOK
...I think the last page is just under the wing there! It made a great papier-mâché!
ARRGGHHH! I can't take it anymore!

I've got to get away from this sewer rat!
RRIP

WAHHHHHH!
Not quite how I expected the escape plan to pan out, but it'll do!

MY FAVOURITE PLACE
BEA
The Playpark
I'm gonna hurl.
Hyik-hyik!
SANDPAPER
Going up!
COUGH!
CHOKE!
My pals are loadsa fun!

THE FANTASTICALLY FUNNY FATTY
Q - WHAT COLOUR IS A BURP? A - BURPLE.
Q - What is black, white, green and bumpy? A - A pickle wearing a tuxedo.
Q - What do you call cheese that doesn't belong to you? A - Nacho cheese.
Q - What do you get from a pampered cow? A - Spoilt milk.
Q - DID YOU HEAR THE JOKE ABOUT PEANUT BUTTER? A - I'M NOT TELLING YOU. YOU MIGHT SPREAD IT.
Ha! That's really Funny.
That's pretty good, Fatty.
Q - What do you call ham you really miss? A - Pork-you-pine.
Hahahahaha!
You're so Funny, Fatty!

I WONDER WHAT'S UNDER...
FRED'S BED?

DRAMA CLASS-
Today, children, we will be rehearsing the Scottish play!
The Scottish play? It says 'Macbeth' here!
MACBETH By Some Guy
Wingle, wangle, save this show from a tangle!
Huh? What are you doing?
The Scottish play is cursed! Should you say the title out loud, you must spin three times and use the rhyme I just did to rid the bad luck!
Bad luck, eh? Just 'cos I said 'Macbeth'?
H.H.

Wingle, wangle, save this show from a tangle!
Ho-ho!
MACB
Macb-
No you don't. And you can say 'goodbye' to a part too!
Harrumph! Grumpy, ol' teacher. I'm off to find someone who will appreciate my actin'!

Coo - wonder if I can get a part in a play here?
Stage Door
ye Globe theatre Olde London towne
all next weeke: Mr. Willie Shakespeare's New Comedie "Carry On Hamlet"
Stage Door
'Ello! Don't mind me - I'm an actor...
BUT-
And stay out! I've seen less ham in a pig farm!
Stage Door
Worra cheek.
SPLUTTCHH!!
YUCK!
Poor soul - have a penny.
There's no need, I'm not a beggar... hang on, is this coin gold?
Woe, woe, and thrice woe! I am just a poor beggar. I'm totally skint, but making a mint!
SOON-
ye Globe Boxe office
Two shillings per seate
Woo-hoo! Enough money to see the show! An' they said I couldn't act!

Hur-hur-hur! I'm right at the front – I'll just need to get a part now!
Nexte Performance in about ye half hour (if ye naughty Actors be not in ye local pub)
When shall we three meet again In thunder, lightning or in rain?
There's something funny about those witches...
LATER-
They met me in the day of success...
Wait a minute! Those witches had beards!
HARDLY A MINUTE, FRED! THAT WAS FOUR SCENES AGO! BEANO ED.
Thou'rt mad... GLERK!
You've got a beard too, Lady Macbeth!
You're ruining thy play.
You're supposed to be a lady... ugly sister more like!
Thou GERROFF!
Yeeps!
A soft landing at least!
Ye Actors' Costumes

You seen an annoying, little nit round 'ere?
Sorry, sir.
You can't be talking about me, surely?
Ye Back of Ye Stage
'Ello. Who are you, then?
I'm Banquo's ghost!
Sheesh! You're not much of a ghost looking like that. Here – have this sheet!
Glumphle!
To Ye Stage
There you go – you're on now, mate!
Christopher Marlowe Waz 'ere 1601
I have a strange infirmity... OOF!
Sorry!
Whoops! What's this?
Look out – he's behind you! Ho-ho!

I thought Macbeth was supposed to be a tragedy – I hadn't realised it's a panto! Hur-hur!
This play is cursed!
MACBETH By Jon Scieszka
By that little demon!
Uh-oh!
I'm outta here – the company of players is gettin' ugly!
You're no oil painting, thyself!
Hey, you don't suppose Macbeth's thought to be cursed 'cos of little, old me... do you, readers?
Don't worry, Fred – you're secret's safe with us! Ho-ho!
READER.
MACBETH By William Shakespeare

MINNIE the MINX

A competition to fly without an engine? I am SO into that!
UNPOWERED FLYING CONTEST
AT BEANOTOWN PARK TODAY

It would be BRILLIANT to fly - so I will!
FLAP!
FLAP!
FLAP!
FLAP!
SKIP!
HOP!

ZZZ
ZZZ
ZZZ?
SWIPE
Uh?

CLUNK!
OOH!

Minnie? What are you up to?
Cackles!

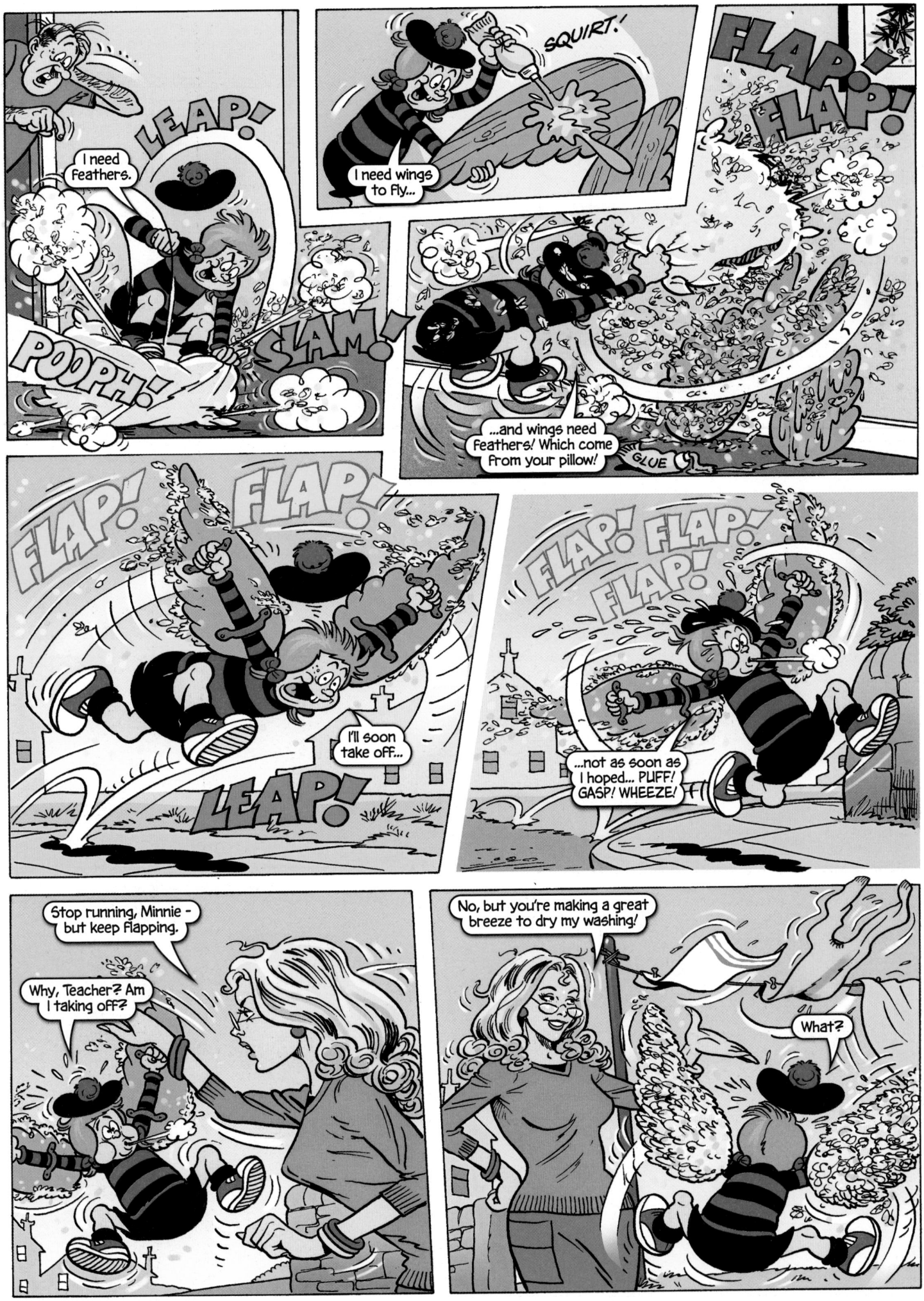
I need feathers.
LEAP!
POOPH!
SLAM!
SQUIRT!
I need wings to fly...
FLAP!
FLAP!
...and wings need feathers! Which come from your pillow!
GLUE
FLAP!
FLAP!
I'll soon take off...
LEAP!
FLAP!
FLAP!
FLAP!
...not as soon as I hoped... PUFF! GASP! WHEEZE!
Stop running, Minnie - but keep flapping.
Why, Teacher? Am I taking off?
No, but you're making a great breeze to dry my washing!
What?

Thanks, Minnie.
I am not amused!
STOMP!

WHACK!
THUD!
BASH!
I always get nervous when Minnie makes things.
And she's always making a bloomin' noise.

Who needs an engine when you've got pedal power?

RATTLE!
Leggies to full pedal!
ZOOM!
TAKE-OFF RAMP

Up and... we're off!
ZOOM!

I'm Flying! I'm Flying!
PEDALLING LIKE CRAZY

I'm stalling!
And I'm falling!
SPLASH!
And we're soaking!
That was ACE! Can I do it again?
Minnie, we'll help you fly!
You will? You're not so bad after all, Dad!
There. That's much better!
FLAP!
You are NOT funny, Dad!
SPIN!
That'll keep her out of mischief!
H. HARRISON.

BILLY WHIZZ
I've got a great challenge ahead!
CLICK!
On your marks, get set - bake!
I'll need a mixing bowl.
ZOOM!
In go the flour and the sugar!
BUMP!
FLING!
CRAB!
CRACK!
CRACK!
CRACK!
CRACK!
WHISK

SPLATCH!
Into the tin, it goes!

Time to go!
FWOOSH!
NICK BRENNAN

ITALY
SICILY
ZOOOOOOOM!

TOOT!
ZZZZIPP!
MOUNT ETNA

BLOOPS

Baked to a turn!
SPLOOP!

HOOOFF!
FWIP!!!
CLIK!
48 seconds!
RING!
BINK!
It's official - I can cook faster than a microwave oven!

HERE, IN ACACIA AVENUE, IS LITTLE ERIC...
ZZZZZZZZ!
HO! I SAID, "HERE IS LITTLE ERIC"! WAKE UP!
I heard you. Go away. I'm sleeping.
THAT'S CHARMING, THAT IS. AND I WAS GOING TO WARN YOU THAT YOU'RE LATE FOR SCHOOL, BUT I SHAN'T BOTHER NOW. I'LL SULK INSTEAD.
Can't stand it when caption writers go all moody. I'll just have a shower...
TUG!
WHINE!
It's c-c-cold!
Crumbs! It's REALLY cold! My windows are all frosted!

THUD! THUD! THUD!
WHUMP!
EEPS!
Yikes!
BANANAMAN! IN THE BIG CHILL!
Even the phone sounds cold.
BRRRRRR!
'Tis Chief O'Reilly.
Oh really?
NO, O'REILLY! GET BANANAMAN HERE NOW!
If he needs Bananaman, I need a banana...
...except all my bananas have frozen solid!
TAP! TAP

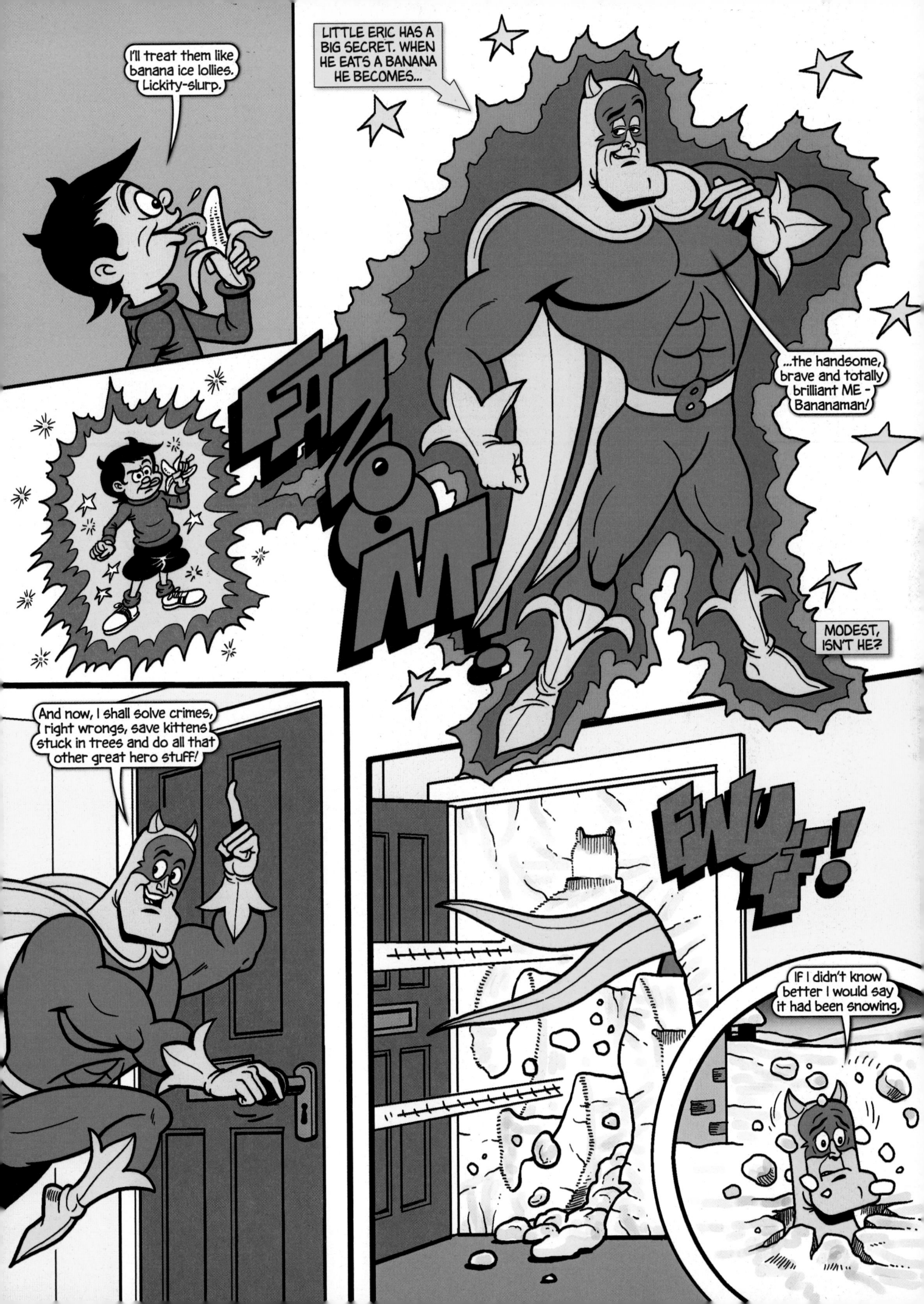
I'll treat them like banana ice lollies. Lickity-slurp.
LITTLE ERIC HAS A BIG SECRET. WHEN HE EATS A BANANA HE BECOMES...
FIZZ
POP
...the handsome, brave and totally brilliant ME - Bananaman!
MODEST, ISN'T HE?
And now, I shall solve crimes, right wrongs, save kittens stuck in trees and do all that other great hero stuff!
FWUP!
IF I didn't know better I would say it had been snowing.

Aha! There's the cop shop...
POLICE H.Q.
...but where's Chief O'Reilly? And why has he got a pile of dreadful old clothes on his desk?
This isn't a pile of old clothes, you blue dimwit. I'm wearing layers to stay warm!
Sorry, Chiefy.
CHIEFY
My lads are all snow-bound. You need to find out what caused the big freeze.
Well, using my super-powers of deduction I'd say it was the temperature but I'll investigate.
I'm HOT on the trail of this COLD-hearted baddie.
KERASH!
Sure, I really wish he would use the door. So I do.
A crowd? Out in this cold? I wonder why?

HOT WATER BOTTLES
£5 EACH
SPECIAL OFFER: 2 FOR £15
YES, FOLKS, THAT'S THE PLOT EXPLAINED!
General, it's 'Nana-knickers. Do you think he's on to our cunning scheme to make a hot-water bottle fortune by turning the weather cold?
Don't worry, Weatherman. I've got a plan so cunning you could give it a moustache and call it Einstein.
Er, are you sure this will fool him?
I'd like a word with you two...
Oh, crumbs...
Have you seen any unusual goings-on, or any naughty villains? They're probably around where you least expect them.
A bit like your brain cells, then? Nope, we haven't seen anybody.
SCOOSH!
Pity. In that case I'll just have a couple of these, please?
SCOOSH!
You muscled-up mug. You'll...

Burst them?
I think you just did.
POP!
POP!
DUNT!
DUNT!
OOF!
OW!
It must be cold! Their moustaches have fallen off!
Hang on. It's General Blight and Weatherman. These two villains must have caused the freeze.
The shame of it. Caught by this nitwit... again!
It's the COOLER for you two. We'll FREEZE your bank accounts while you CHILL out in here. It's n-ICE to get you behind bars again!
THE NICK
We'll do our time - just stop with the rotten puns, ok?
MILK
BRIGHTY

ROGER the DODGER
Morning, Roger. I've got a joke for you. What's a mower for?
I don't know, Dad. What's a mower for?
Gardening, Roger! Ha-ha! You'll need these too!
Harrumph! Rotten Dad-joke. Walked right into that one, didn't I?
And this garden's really overgrown! It's going to take more effort than I like to put in... like any at all! I need a dodge!
50 -
Explain this to me again...
I told you - it's simple...
BEANOTOWN SPORTS CLUB
...we sign up to a sports club.
Which one?
SIGN ON! HOCKEY AMERICAN FOOTBALL CRICKET BASEBALL
All of them!
Right. What now?

Now for the next part of my dodge – we need a bone.
Where'll we get one of those?
SNORE
Right there!
Eeps! That's Gnasher – we can't steal a bone from him!
Not 'steal' – 'trade'. For this hockey stick.
Coo – that's brave!
Very brave. I'll be right behind you, mate!
It's like defusing a bomb!
Be careful not to set this one off then!
SLIDE!
Uh-oh!
SWEAT!
SWEAT!
POP!

DRIP!
GNASH!
YEOW!
GNASH!
GNASH!
ARGH!
I'm suddenly glad we got all that padded sports' gear.
It was worth a gnashing to get this! A bone's just what I need!
BACK IN DENNIS' GARDEN -
Gnuh?
The next stage of my dodge comes here!
Huh?
BEANOTOWN ARCHAEOLOGICAL SOCIETY

INSIDE -
Crikey! I've never seen a bone like this. Where did you find it?
Dug it up out of my garden, so I did.
These teeth marks must've been made by some fearsome, incredible prehistoric beast! This could be quite a discovery!
AND -
Who would've thought there'd be people happy to dig the garden, eh?
Nice one, Roger!
So... find anything?
No more of your bones... I'm afraid this find is going to remain a mystery.
SOON -
Here you go, Roger. We archaeologists return everything to normal once we're finished - so no one will know we've been.
Ta. Sorry your team couldn't find anything else.
That was a truly audacious dodge, Roger.

BUT -
SNIFF! SNIFF!
SNIFF!
My bone's somewhere here, I can smell it!
BUT -
ROAR!
Think I'll catch some zzzzs.
Yeah - no work for us. An afternoon nap sounds like a great idea.
Wassat?? Who cut short my nap?
Problem, Dad? Don't you like the job I did on the garden?
Not really, no!
Aw, no! Gnasher's dug the whole garden up!
Don't blame Gnasher! You'll be needing these tools again, my lad!
Still gno bone. I was sure it was here!

PUP PARADE
BEANOTOWN LOCAL DUMP
Not again!
Morning... I think!
What an improvement, Pug!
NIGEL PARKINSON.

This happens to us every week!
Bin day!

That's it, Pups. I'm fed up being thrown out with the rubbish. Time to say goodbye to the bin and find somewhere else to live!

SO -
It's like a home from home.
This entrance is a little on the narrow side.
You mean your bum is a little on the wide side!

BUT THAT NIGHT -

THE NEXT MORNING -
Okay. Time for plan B.
But I love papier mâché!

LATER THAT DAY -
RUBBISH PLEASE TAKE
Look, 'Enry. That hammock will be the perfect thing for us Pups!
Great idea, Spotty!

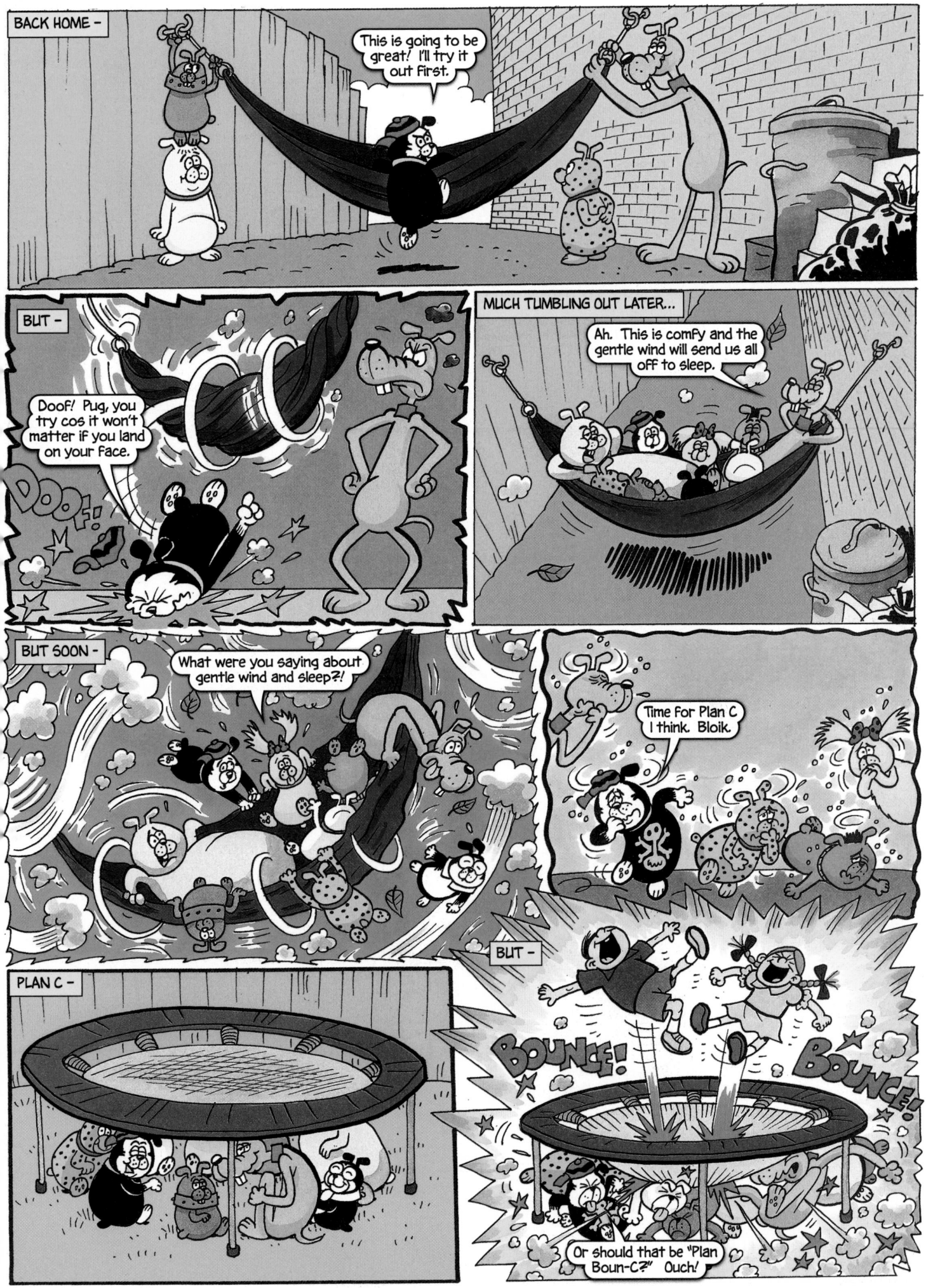
BACK HOME -
This is going to be great! I'll try it out first.
BUT -
Doof! Pug, you try cos it won't matter if you land on your face.
DOOF!
MUCH TUMBLING OUT LATER...
Ah. This is comfy and the gentle wind will send us all off to sleep.
BUT SOON -
What were you saying about gentle wind and sleep?!
Time for Plan C I think. Bloik.
BUT -
BOUNCE!
BOUNCE!
Or should that be "Plan Boun-C?" Ouch!
PLAN C -

Back to the bin, Bones?
Sigh. Back to the bin, Pups.
Ho-ho! Plan D coming up!
WET CEMENT
This bin is going NOWHERE now!
NEXT BIN DAY –
Gnnngh! This bin's not shifting.
Tee-hee!
They'll never shift us now that we've got our names in the Beanotown walk of fame!
MANFRID
PEEPS
BLOTTY
PUG
TUBBY
BONES
'ENRY
SNIFFY
WIGGY

BONKERS BIRTHDAY OFFER FOR THE BEANO® FANS!

A FREE interactive digital issue for every reader at www.Beano.com/BNAN2

15 ISSUES FOR ONLY £15

GR8 REASONS TO SIGN UP!

- Never miss an issue of your favourite comic.
- Get your copy sent to you before it's in the shops!
- Special subscriber offers!
- Get the latest laughs, jokes and pranks before anyone else!
- Includes all cover promotions! Post free delivery.
- Save on the shop price.

WHAT TO DO...

Ask a parent or guardian to help.
Visit: **www.Beano.com/BNAN2**
Call **0800 318 846** 8am-9pm, 7 days.
When ordering please quote code BNAN2

UNDISPUTED
IT'S THE CHEAPEST AND FASTEST WAY TO GET BRITAIN'S FAVOURITE COMIC!

15 issues for £15 offer available to UK residents. Overseas residents qualify for a 20% discount on our Direct Debit and one year subscription terms by quoting BNAN2. Please call: +44 1382 575580 or visit our website www.beano.com/subscribe for more details. The Beano ® © and associated characters TM© DC Thomson & Co., Ltd. 2012. Offer ends 30 March 2013.

THE BEANO®
COMIC GIFT COLLECTION
WWW.BEANO.COM
A selection of gifts that celebrates over 70 years of fun from The Beano.
COLLECTABLE FIGURINES & ARTWORK
WE'RE ARMED AND VERY, VERY DANGEROUS! HEH-HEH!
WATER
ROTTEN TOMATOES
THE BEANO
DENNIS THE MENACE AND GNASHER
DENNIS the MENACE 1974
GNASHER
THE Beano BOOK 1977
TOYS & GAMES
BEANO
Dandy
CLOTHES & ACCESSORIES
MENACE
More gifts online
WWW.BEANO.COM
or call 0800 318 846 (UK)
Overseas call +44 1382 575580
Lines open 8am – 9pm, 7 days
email - shop@beano.com
Scan the QR code with your smartphone for direct access to The Beano Shop Online.
The Beano ® © and associated characters TM© DC Thomson & Co., Ltd. 2012.

2013 BEANO® SURVEY

£200 IN CASH PRIZES TO BE WON!

OUR CUSTOMERS AND READERS ARE IMPORTANT TO US AND YOUR OPINIONS REALLY MATTER. WE WANT THE BEANO ANNUAL TO PROVIDE THE PERFECT READ AND EXPERIENCE, SO PLEASE TAKE THE TIME TO FILL IN THIS SURVEY TO LET US KNOW IF WE ARE GETTING THIS RIGHT.

FILLING IN OUR QUESTIONNAIRE IS EASY

IT'S FASTER AND EASIER TO GO TO
WWW.COMPLETEASURVEY.CO.UK/BEANOANNUAL2013
ALTERNATIVELY COMPLETE THE PAPER COPY AND POST TO: 2013 BEANO ANNUAL SURVEY FREEPOST RSKR-YGJG-XERH CONSUMER INSIGHT DEPARTMENT 80 KINGSWAY EAST DUNDEE DD4 8SL (NO STAMP IS REQUIRED)
IF YOU ARE UNDER 16 PLEASE ASK AN ADULT'S PERMISSION BEFORE COMPLETING THE SURVEY. ALL ONLINE AND POSTAL SURVEYS RETURNED BY 1ST MARCH 2013 WILL BE ENTERED INTO A DRAW TO WIN A TOP PRIZE OF £100 AND 2 PRIZES OF £50!

IF YOU WOULD LIKE TO BE ENTERED INTO THE PRIZE DRAW, PLEASE FILL IN YOUR DETAILS BELOW (OPTIONAL)

TITLE ..... FIRST NAME ..... LAST NAME .....

ADDRESS .....

.....

.....

POSTCODE ..... EMAIL ADDRESS .....

YOUR REPLIES TO THIS QUESTIONNAIRE WILL BE TREATED WITH THE STRICTEST CONFIDENCE AND USED FOR STATISTICAL PURPOSES ONLY. HOWEVER, FROM TIME TO TIME THE PUBLISHERS OF THIS ANNUAL, DC THOMSON & CO LTD AND CAREFULLY SELECTED THIRD PARTIES MAY WISH TO CONTACT YOU VIA POST OR EMAIL WITH OFFERS AND PROMOTIONS. IF YOU WOULD PREFER NOT TO BE CONTACTED PLEASE TICK THE RELEVANT BOX(ES).

☐ I DO NOT WANT TO BE CONTACTED BY THE PUBLISHER OF THIS ANNUAL, DC THOMSON & CO LTD.

☐ I DO NOT WANT TO BE CONTACTED BY THIRD PARTIES.

DID YOU BUY THE BEANO ANNUAL OR RECEIVE IT AS GIFT FROM SOMEONE?

☐ I BOUGHT IT
☐ I RECEIVED IT AS A GIFT (PLEASE PROCEED TO SECTION B)

A PLEASE ONLY ANSWER THE FOLLOWING QUESTIONS IF YOU BOUGHT THIS ANNUAL

IN WHICH MONTH DID YOU PURCHASE THE BEANO ANNUAL?

☐ JANUARY ☐ FEBRUARY ☐ MARCH
☐ APRIL ☐ MAY ☐ JUNE
☐ JULY ☐ AUGUST ☐ SEPTEMBER
☐ OCTOBER ☐ NOVEMBER ☐ DECEMBER

WHERE DID YOU BUY THE BEANO ANNUAL?

☐ SUPERMARKET
☐ BOOK SHOP
☐ HIGH STREET STORE
☐ LOCAL NEWSAGENT
☐ DIRECT FROM DC THOMSON
☐ ONLINE
OTHER (PLEASE TELL US).....

WHAT MADE YOU BUY THE BEANO ANNUAL?
(PLEASE TICK ALL ANSWERS THAT APPLY)

☐ I READ THE BEANO COMIC
☐ I BUY THE BEANO COMIC
☐ I SUBSCRIBE TO THE BEANO COMIC
☐ I WATCH DENNIS AND GNASHER ON TV
☐ I HAVE BEANO MERCHANDISE (E.G. TOYS/CLOTHING)
☐ I HAVE VISITED THE BEANO WEBSITE
☐ I HAVE DOWNLOADED THE BEANO DIGITAL EDITION
☐ THE BEANO CHARACTERS
☐ I WAS ATTRACTED BY THE BEANO COVER
☐ THE PRICE
☐ I SAW IT ADVERTISED IN A MAGAZINE/NEWSPAPER/WEBSITE
☐ I'VE BOUGHT THE BEANO ANNUAL BEFORE
☐ I SAW IT ADVERTISED IN A BROCHURE I RECEIVED FROM DC THOMSON
☐ I BUY THE BEANO ANNUAL EVERY YEAR
☐ I WANTED TO KEEP UP/ESTABLISH A FAMILY TRADITION
☐ THERE WAS A PRICE PROMOTION
☐ I WANTED TO INTRODUCE SOMEONE TO THE BEANO

OTHER (PLEASE TELL US).....

DID YOU BUY THE BEANO ANNUAL AS A GIFT FOR SOMEONE?

☐ YES ☐ NO

IF YES, WAS THE GIFT FOR...

☐ AN ADULT ☐ A CHILD

AND WAS THAT PERSON...

☐ A SON OR DAUGHTER
☐ A GRANDCHILD
☐ A SIBLING
☐ ANOTHER CHILD
☐ A FRIEND
☐ A SPOUSE OR PARTNER
☐ A PARENT
☐ A GRANDPARENT
OTHER (PLEASE TELL US).....

HAVE YOU BOUGHT THE BEANO ANNUAL BEFORE?

☐ YES ☐ NO

IF YES, FOR HOW LONG HAVE YOU BEEN BUYING THE BEANO ANNUAL?

☐ 1-2 YEARS ☐ 3-5 YEARS
☐ 6-10 YEARS ☐ 10 YEARS +

HAVE YOU EVER BOUGHT ANY OTHER ANNUALS THIS YEAR?

☐ YES ☐ NO

IF SO, PLEASE TELL US WHICH ONES.....

.....

HAVE YOU BOUGHT MORE OR LESS ANNUALS THIS YEAR?

☐ MORE ☐ THE SAME ☐ LESS

CAN YOU SAY WHY?.....

.....

B PLEASE ONLY ANSWER THE FOLLOWING QUESTIONS IF YOU ARE THE MAIN READER OF THIS ANNUAL

ARE YOU THE MAIN READER OF THE BEANO ANNUAL?

☐ YES ☐ NO (PLEASE PROCEED TO SECTION C)

HAVE YOU READ/RECEIVED THIS ANNUAL BEFORE?

☐ YES ☐ NO

HOW LONG HAVE YOU BEEN READING THE BEANO ANNUAL FOR?

☐ 1-2 YEARS ☐ 3-5 YEARS
☐ 6-10 YEARS ☐ 10 YEARS +

THINKING ABOUT THE BEANO ANNUAL AND CHARACTERS, WHICH OF THE FOLLOWING APPLY?
(PLEASE TICK ALL ANSWERS THAT APPLY)

☐ I READ THE BEANO COMIC
☐ I BUY THE BEANO COMIC
☐ I SUBSCRIBE TO THE BEANO COMIC
☐ I WATCH DENNIS & GNASHER ON TV
☐ I HAVE BEANO MERCHANDISE (E.G TOYS/CLOTHING)
☐ I HAVE VISITED THE BEANO WEBSITE
☐ I HAVE DOWNLOADED THE BEANO DIGITAL EDITION

HAVE YOU READ/RECEIVED ANY OTHER ANNUALS THIS YEAR?

☐ YES ☐ NO

IF SO, PLEASE TELL US WHICH ONES.....

.....

HAVE YOU READ A DIGITAL EDITION OF AN ANNUAL?

☐ YES
☐ NO BUT I WOULD CONSIDER IT
☐ NO AND I WOULD NOT CONSIDER IT

IF YES, PLEASE TELL US WHICH DIGITAL EDITION ANNUALS YOU HAVE READ

.....

C ABOUT YOU

THINKING ABOUT TECHNOLOGY, WHICH OF THE FOLLOWING DEVICES DO YOU OWN?

☐ iPHONE ☐ SMARTPHONE (EXCLUDING iPHONE)
☐ iPAD ☐ TABLET PC (EXCLUDING iPAD)
☐ KINDLE ☐ E-READER (EXCLUDING KINDLE)

ARE YOU?

☐ MALE ☐ FEMALE

PLEASE TELL US YOUR AGE...

☐ UNDER 7 ☐ 7-10 ☐ 11-14 ☐ 15-19
☐ 20-24 ☐ 25-34 ☐ 35-44 ☐ 45-54
☐ 55-64 ☐ 65-74 ☐ 75+

WHERE DO YOU LIVE?

☐ SE ENGLAND ☐ SW ENGLAND ☐ LONDON
☐ EAST OF ENGLAND ☐ EAST MIDLANDS ☐ WEST MIDLANDS
☐ YORKS & HUMB ☐ NE ENGLAND ☐ NW ENGLAND
☐ SCOTLAND ☐ WALES ☐ N IRELAND
☐ EIRE
☐ OVERSEAS (IF SO, PLEASE TELL US WHERE)

.....

IF YOU LIVE IN THE UK, PLEASE TELL US YOUR POSTCODE

.....

THANK YOU FOR TAKING THE TIME TO FILL IN THIS SURVEY. YOUR COMMENTS ARE VERY MUCH APPRECIATED! GOOD LUCK IN THE PRIZE DRAW!

Number 13
Mum, do I have to go to school in this weather?
Yes, you do, Boris.
But all this sunlight is bad for us monsters. Look what it did to cousin Vlad.
You're not kidding... I was 5 minutes late getting home from vampiring all night and the sun did this!
I'll fix that nasty old sun.
ZAP!
There. A lovely downpour. That's much nicer.
I suppose.
It's not better for me. I can't see a thing with all this wet fur in my eyes.
AAAAAAAAAAAHHH!
Suppose I'd better get to school. Hi, Postie. Hi, Tiddles.

Some of the kids at my school are a bit mean.
Gimme your lunch, shrimp.
Gibber.

I s-suppose you w-want my l-lunch as well?
Hand it over, weirdo.

Okay, here you go!
HURFF!
'O'-TYPE

You sorted him out. Well done, Boris.
What did I do?
FAINT

Did you do this, Boris? You bad lad.

We'll have to get your Father in. What will he say about this?
#13

Hello, Teacher. What seems to be the problem?
Uh?
Whine... But... You're...
Are you all right? You don't look well.
WAAAAAAAAAAAAAAAHHH!
What a strange man. Was it something I said?
No bully and no Teacher! Well done, Boris. You're our hero! You rock!
My schoolmates like me! Dad, can we have a sleepover? Please?
We've never had one in our family before, but... okay.
And now I know why we've never had a sleepover in our family before...

HELP!
NYEEE-HEEE-HEEEE!
EEPS!
HOWL!
It's because none of your pals will get any sleep. Myah-hah-hah!
GIBBER!
Can I get you anything?
Heh-heh-heh!

MINNIE THE MINX
Tum-ti-tum...
Aha! There's my old Dad!
DAD!
What have you got there? Don't Fire, whatever it is!
SMILE!
FLASH!
YIKES!
Oh. She was only taking a picture. What a relief!
SKIP!
SKIP!
SKIP!
Ooh, donuts. Slobber.
MUNCH!
MUNCH!
MUNCH
BAG OF DONUTS
My old mate, Fatty Fudge, enjoying a little donut snack.

FLASH!
Wotcher, Fatty!
BAG OF DONUTS
Sneak Minx attack? Or just a photo?
NEXT...
FRUIT
HYIK-HYIK! There's my Teacher...
Must get some healthy food...
MELO
FLASH!
YOOHOO!
EEPS! MINNIE!
Minnie, what was that all about?
Just taking a few pictures!
SKIP!
SKIP!
Well, she might have been a pest with her camera but I'm happy she's got a hobby.
If she's given up minxing for photography I'm happy.
SKIP!
SKIP!
And at least she didn't use her catapult.
Given up minxing? There's a reason I wanted these pics...

Given up her catty? No bloomin' chance!
We should have known better!
SPLAT!
SPLAT!
SPLAT!
NIP!
SPIN!
SPLAT!
TWANG!
TOMATOES
SPLAT!
Heh-heh! I just wanted a bit of target practice!
KEN.H.HARRISON.

MY FAVOURITE PLACE
BALLBOY
The Ball pool
On me head!
On your head, your feet, your elbows, your nose... they're everywhere!
This is BRILLIANT!
It's fun for the spectators, too.

STINKING RICH
A FOUL FABLE
ONCE UPON A TIME, A CUTE LITTLE BABY NAMED RICHARD WAS BORN.
Goo-goo!
HIS MUM WAS SO PROUD - AND ALL THE NURSES SAID HE WAS A BEAUTIFUL BABY.
What a beautiful baby.
SEE? TOLD YOU.
BUT NOT EVERYTHING WAS HOW IT SEEMED WITH THIS LITTLE BABY...
Gnnn...
...BECAUSE HE HAD A SQUEAKY TUMMY.
FFFRRRPPPP
AND HE WASN'T HALF PONGY.
AND HIS PONGY HABITS CARRIED ON THROUGH HIS LIFE. AT NURSERY...
PP

...THINGS WERE NO BETTER.

AT SCHOOL, HE COULDN'T STOP - AND PEOPLE WERE STARTING TO NOTICE.
Oxygen! Need oxygen!

AND WHEN IT CAME TIME TO ASK A GIRL OUT ON A DATE...

...HE DIDN'T HAVE ANY SUCCESS THERE. EVEN THE RHUBARB WILTED FROM HIS TROUSER TRUMPS.

BUT A TV TALENT SCOUT SPOTTED OUR PAL, RICH...
Wanna be a star?
Not interested.

For THIS much?
I'm interested!

SOON HE WAS ON A TALENT SHOW...

BUT HE GOT NERVOUS...
Lots of people watching...
VERY NERVOUS...
Oh, crumbs. I'm going to...
AND SO HIS TV CAREER ENDED BEFORE IT EVEN STARTED.
KARFOOM
BUT HE WASN'T TOO BOTHERED - BECAUSE HE GOT A HAPPY ENDING...
...MAKING A FORTUNE AS A DEMOLITION EXPERT.
Just call me STINKING RICH!
FRROOOMM

VILE TIMES WITH EVIL EDGAR

Potion in the Ocean!

By Philip Minion

1 **AS a low-level minion in the employ of Doctor E. L. Pumpshoffen, otherwise known as Evil Edgar, I was used to working in the cramped conditions of his underground laboratory.**

However, as I swept the path which ran through the forest of fungus two miles below street level, I had a sudden urge to breathe clean, fresh air again.

3 This glance proved to be my undoing, as I tripped on the next step. The next thing I knew, Edgar was speaking as he grabbed my shoulder in one of his claw-like hands. "What an eager volunteer! You've made my minion crew complete!" he said.

5 The baboons put on a spurt and pedalled furiously, driving our evil master's U-boat around a U-bend and popping us out into the Atlantic a couple of hundred metres below the surface! The Nematode was a swift vessel and we made steady progress towards the West (I shuddered to think of the horrible nature of the experiments which had led Edgar to discover that the baboons pedalled faster whenever Country and Western music was played over the speaker system).

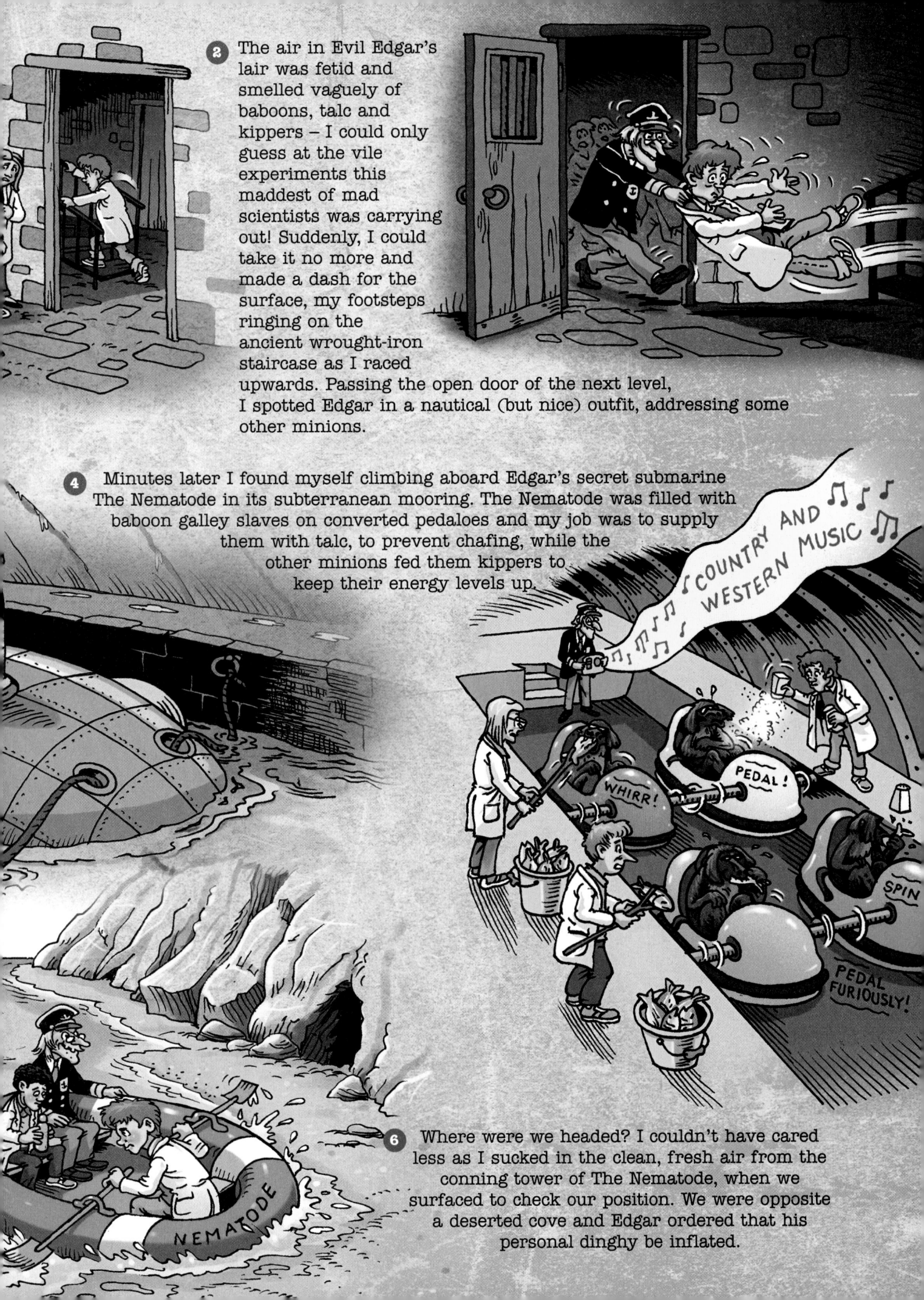

2 The air in Evil Edgar's lair was fetid and smelled vaguely of baboons, talc and kippers – I could only guess at the vile experiments this maddest of mad scientists was carrying out! Suddenly, I could take it no more and made a dash for the surface, my footsteps ringing on the ancient wrought-iron staircase as I raced upwards. Passing the open door of the next level, I spotted Edgar in a nautical (but nice) outfit, addressing some other minions.

4 Minutes later I found myself climbing aboard Edgar's secret submarine The Nematode in its subterranean mooring. The Nematode was filled with baboon galley slaves on converted pedaloes and my job was to supply them with talc, to prevent chafing, while the other minions fed them kippers to keep their energy levels up.

6 Where were we headed? I couldn't have cared less as I sucked in the clean, fresh air from the conning tower of The Nematode, when we surfaced to check our position. We were opposite a deserted cove and Edgar ordered that his personal dinghy be inflated.

7 That task fell to me and with the combination of a sigh of relief that the C&W music was switched off and the fresh air in my lungs, I swiftly had the dinghy in the water. Edgar's eyes were glowing bright and he looked especially evil as I rowed the dinghy toward the beach, accompanied by Clive, another minion, clutching a brightly-coloured test tube.

9 I shuddered at the horror of this revelation - giving creatures with a reputation for suction a taste for blood-sucking was fiendish indeed! Edgar turned angrily towards Clive. "The potion isn't working! The limpets remain limp and lifeless – why are they not bloodthirsty?" he demanded. As Clive struggled for an answer, the water in the rock pool bubbled and frothed before erupting in a fine spume as an enormous crab burst forth.

10 "Far from causing vampirism in limpets the potion's causing gigantism in crustaceans!" exclaimed Clive. When Edgar saw what was behind him, he took off like a geriatric whippet across the sand, leapt into the dinghy and rowed back to The Nematode, leaving me and Clive to face the claws of the crab alone!

8 We alighted on the sand and Edgar grabbed the tube from Clive, before skipping across the beach towards a small rock pool. He looked for all the world like an excited schoolboy – albeit one with the facial features of a demented ferret. I asked Clive what was in the test tube, as Edgar poured its contents into the rock pool, and he turned pale. "Nobody in 'potions' is quite sure of what it will do outside of laboratory conditions," began Clive, nervously, "but Edgar is hoping it will cause vampirism in limpets! Oh, and it's a nice colour!"

11 Fortunately, crab eyesight is poor and it scuttled sideways after the movement of Edgar, grabbing his submarine in one giant claw and using the other as a tin opener.

12 What happened next? Did the killer crustacean end the vile career of Evil Edgar? Who knows? Me and Clive popped up the coast for a cream tea and never looked back!

THE END

GNASHER'S BITE
What a brilliant old war movie, Gnasher.
Gnesh!
Yawn! Time for bed!
THE END
SHORTLY...
ZZZZZZ! BLAART...
Are you ready for the big dog-fight over the Channel, Ginger?
Oh, yes, sir. Not half, sir. We'll give the enemy moggy what-for!
Good luck, Wing Commander Gnasher.
Thank you, sir! Doggy-chocs away and all that!
Moggies at three o'clock, Ginger!
Well, it's only quarter past two. We've got time for a cup of tea first!
MIDDLE OF THE ENGLISH CHANNEL

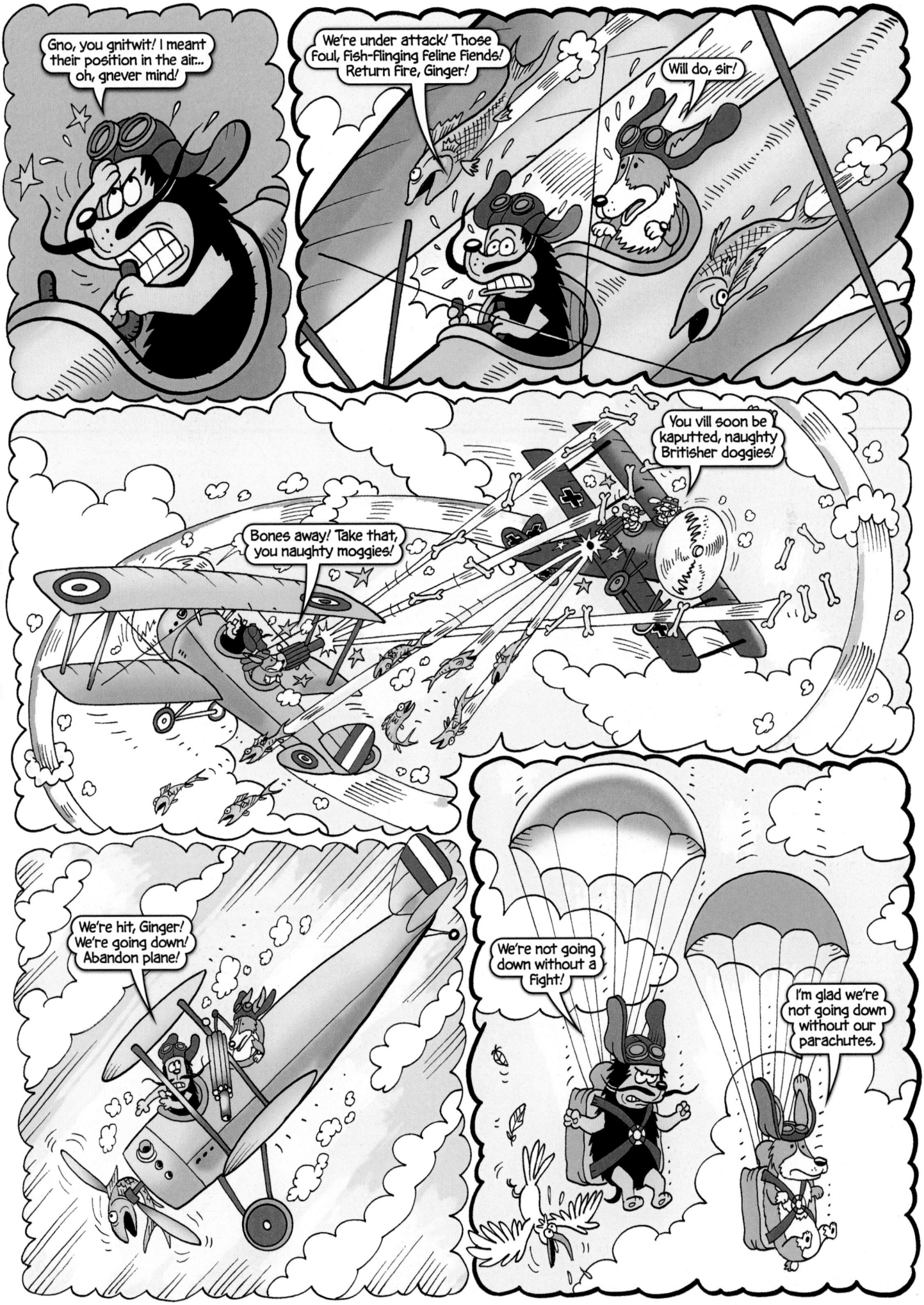
Gno, you gnitwit! I meant their position in the air... oh, gnever mind!
We're under attack! Those foul, fish-flinging feline fiends! Return fire, Ginger!
Will do, sir!
You vill soon be kaputted, naughty Britisher doggies!
Bones away! Take that, you naughty moggies!
We're hit, Ginger! We're going down! Abandon plane!
We're not going down without a fight!
I'm glad we're not going down without our parachutes.

I'm not going down without a fight - or a BITE!
CHOMP!
AAIIIEE! Mine wing! You rotten mutt!
You vill never vin ze var, Herr Doggy!
No moggy ever gets the better of air ace Wing Commander Gnasher!
GNASH!
MYEEEEEKS!
Ve'll see... I mean we'll see about that!
BACK AT BASE...
Splendid effort, old chap. Do have a medal!
YOUR DOG CHUMS NEED
YOU
I can't even start to imagine what he's dreaming about.

The BASH STREET KIDS
Let's have a game of Football!
Super idea! My team against your team!
SLAP!
Excuse me, Danny...
TAP!
...Kevin would like a game.
Huh?
Kevin's only a pebble - how good could he be?
SHRUG!

I've played football with him before!
STAMP!
You mean you kicked him?
NO!
KEEPY-UPPY
He played in goal!
Okay! Kevin can be our goalkeeper.
RUB!
On your head, Wilfrid!
BOOT!
WHEE!
LEAP!
Oops! You need strong neck muscles to be a good header of the ball!
STAGGER!
PLOP!

0-0 AT HALF TIME -
Time for the half time oranges!

I need a little more than that!
You're not kidding!
SQUEEZE!
CHOMP!
GUZZLE!
ICE CREAM
SUCK!

Spotty's got great dribbling skills!
SPIN!
TWIST!

Ha-ha! He's even tied HIMSELF in knots!
TRIP!
ZONK!

IT'S STILL 0-0 IN THE FINAL MINUTE -
I'm right through on goal!
SPIN!

SPIN!

Penalty!
CRUMP!

Are you blind, ref? That was a good tackle!

I'll take the penalty myself.

Straight down the middle usually works!
WHEEE!
BOOT!

BOUNCE!
WHEEE!

Wahey! What a star!

Kevin the pebble for an England cap!
Sigh! I suppose a draw is a fair result!
DS
GENTLE CLAP!

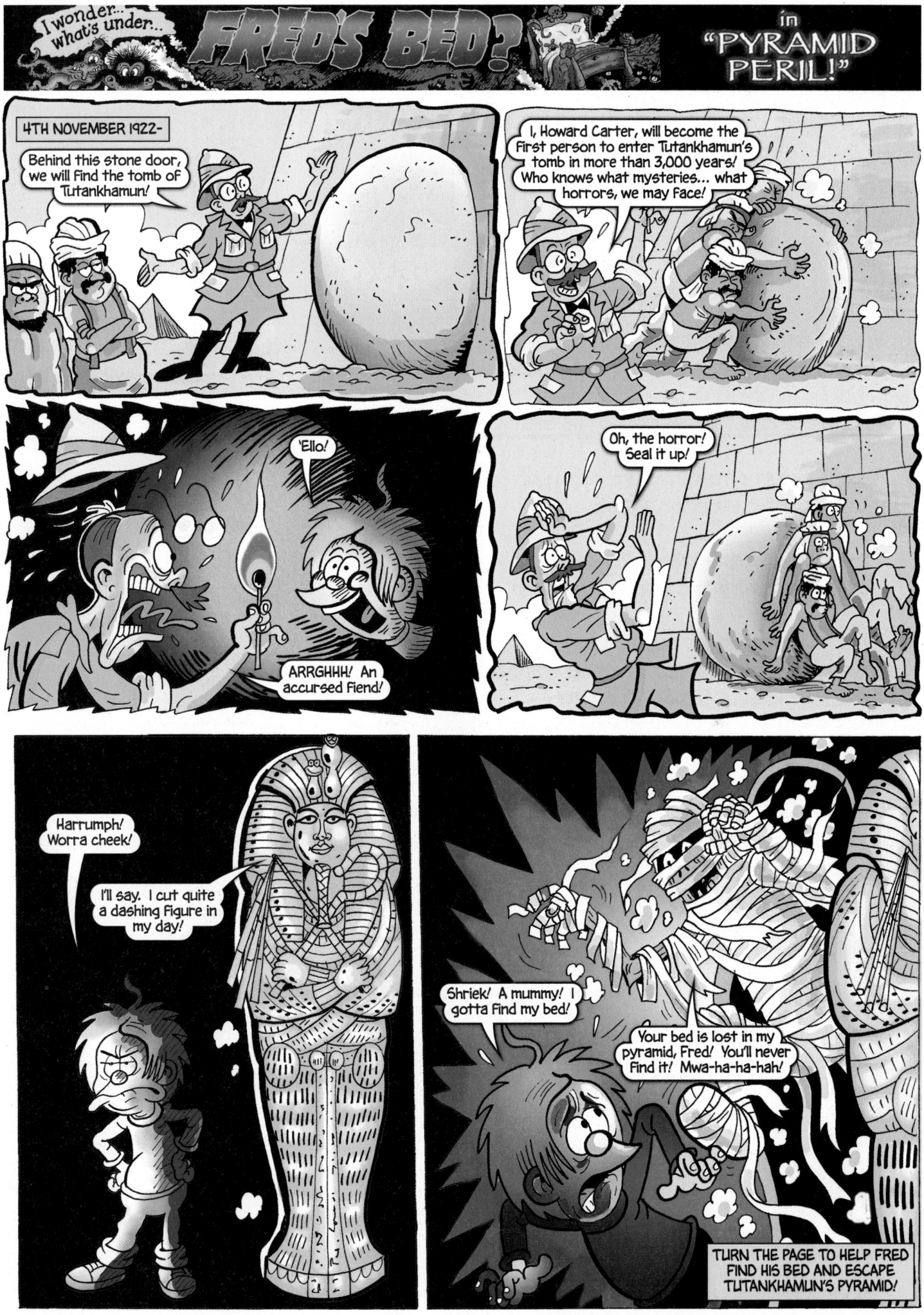
I wonder... what's under...
FRED'S BED?
in "PYRAMID PERIL!"
4TH NOVEMBER 1922-
Behind this stone door, we will find the tomb of Tutankhamun!
I, Howard Carter, will become the first person to enter Tutankhamun's tomb in more than 3,000 years! Who knows what mysteries... what horrors, we may face!
'Ello!
ARRGHHH! An accursed fiend!
Oh, the horror! Seal it up!
Harrumph! Worra cheek!
I'll say. I cut quite a dashing figure in my day!
Shriek! A mummy! I gotta find my bed!
Your bed is lost in my pyramid, Fred! You'll never find it! Mwa-ha-ha-hah!
TURN THE PAGE TO HELP FRED FIND HIS BED AND ESCAPE TUTANKHAMUN'S PYRAMID!

ESCAPE TUTANKHAMUN'S PYRAMID GAME

INSTRUCTIONS

- You will need at least two counters (if you can't find two Egyptian coins, a five pence and a penny will do) and a dice.
- Throw the dice. Highest roll goes first.
- Take it in turns to throw, moving your counter the relevant number of spaces.
- Watch out for the traps and secret passages to help and hinder your path!
- First to reach Fred's bed returns to the present day! The loser(s) will be trapped in Tutankhamun's tomb... Forever!

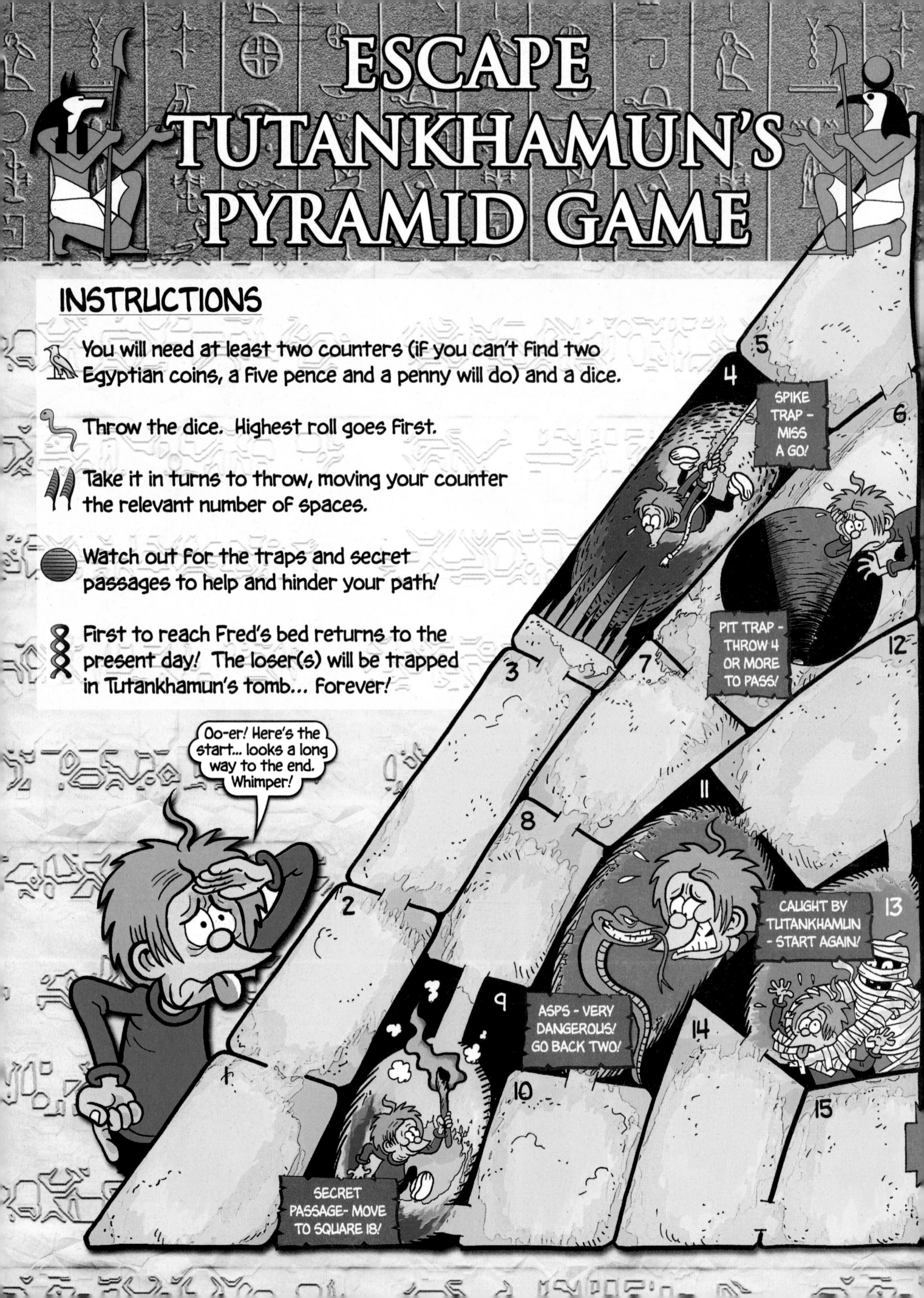

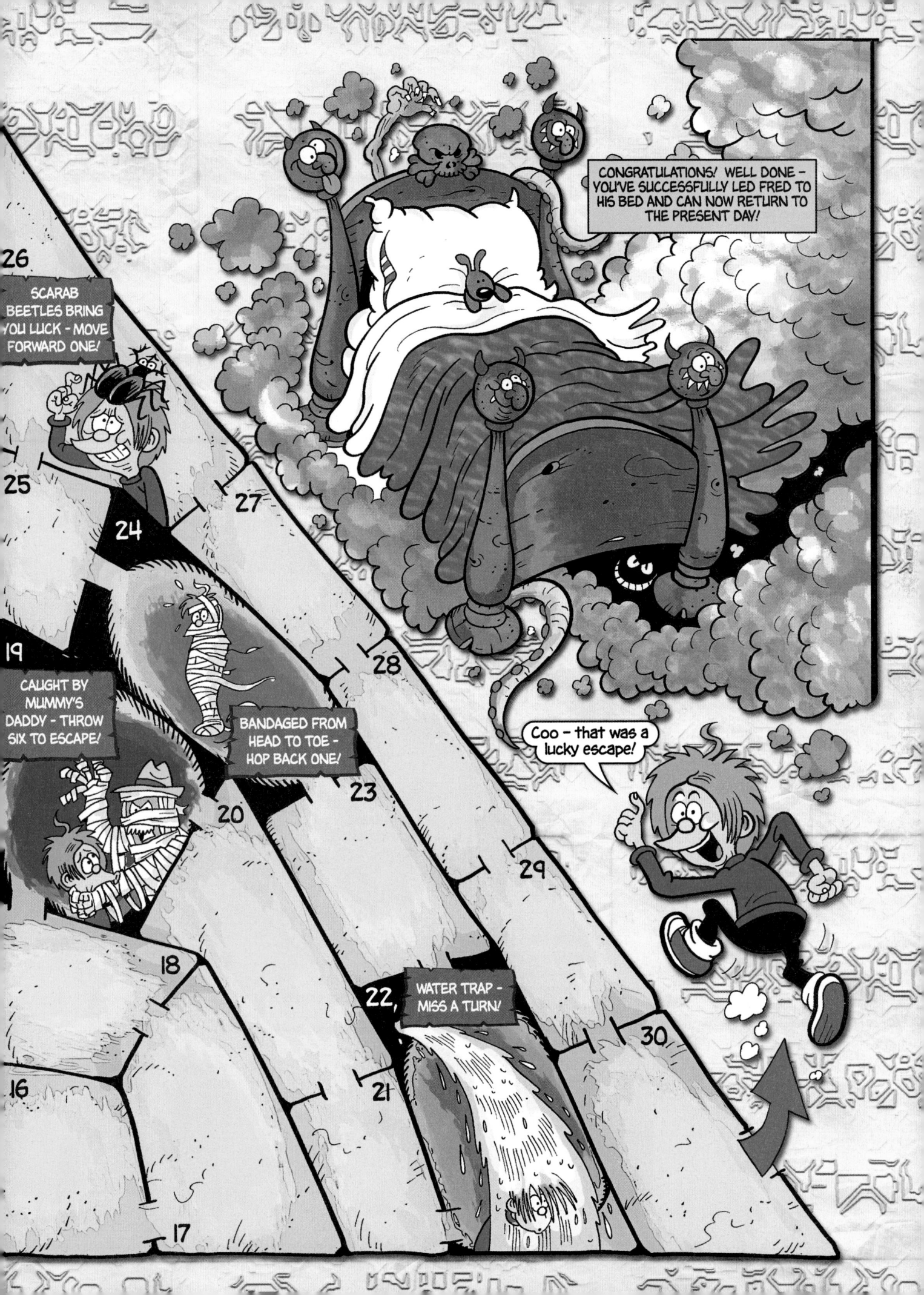
CONGRATULATIONS! WELL DONE – YOU'VE SUCCESSFULLY LED FRED TO HIS BED AND CAN NOW RETURN TO THE PRESENT DAY!
Coo – that was a lucky escape!
26
SCARAB BEETLES BRING YOU LUCK – MOVE FORWARD ONE!
25
24
27
19
28
CAUGHT BY MUMMY'S DADDY – THROW SIX TO ESCAPE!
BANDAGED FROM HEAD TO TOE – HOP BACK ONE!
23
20
29
18
22
WATER TRAP – MISS A TURN!
30
16
21
17

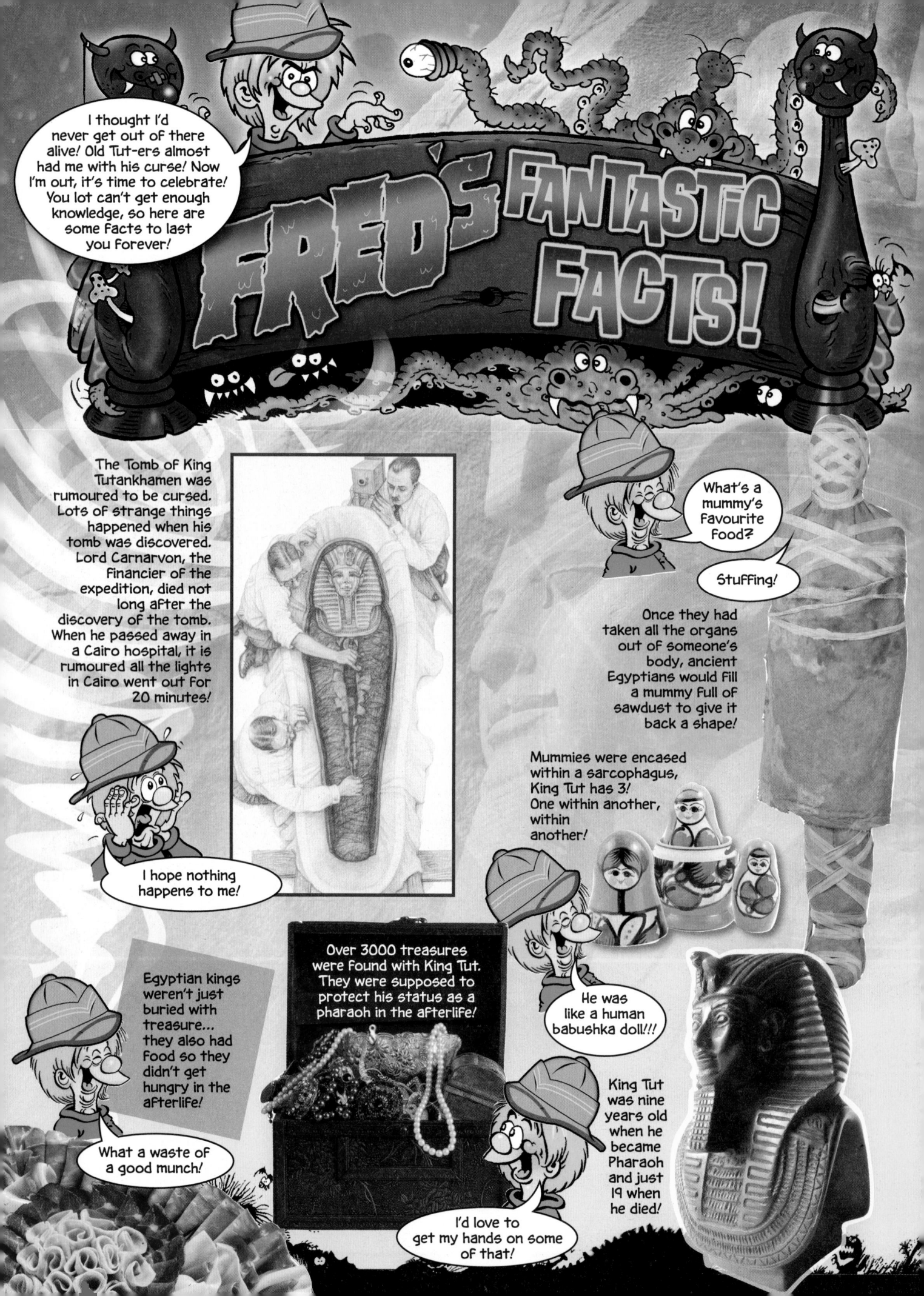
I thought I'd never get out of there alive! Old Tut-ers almost had me with his curse! Now I'm out, it's time to celebrate! You lot can't get enough knowledge, so here are some facts to last you forever!
FRED'S FANTASTIC FACTS!
The Tomb of King Tutankhamen was rumoured to be cursed. Lots of strange things happened when his tomb was discovered. Lord Carnarvon, the financier of the expedition, died not long after the discovery of the tomb. When he passed away in a Cairo hospital, it is rumoured all the lights in Cairo went out for 20 minutes!
I hope nothing happens to me!
What's a mummy's favourite food?
Stuffing!
Once they had taken all the organs out of someone's body, ancient Egyptians would fill a mummy full of sawdust to give it back a shape!
Mummies were encased within a sarcophagus, King Tut has 3! One within another, within another!
He was like a human babushka doll!!!
Egyptian kings weren't just buried with treasure... they also had food so they didn't get hungry in the afterlife!
What a waste of a good munch!
Over 3000 treasures were found with King Tut. They were supposed to protect his status as a pharaoh in the afterlife!
I'd love to get my hands on some of that!
King Tut was nine years old when he became Pharaoh and just 19 when he died!

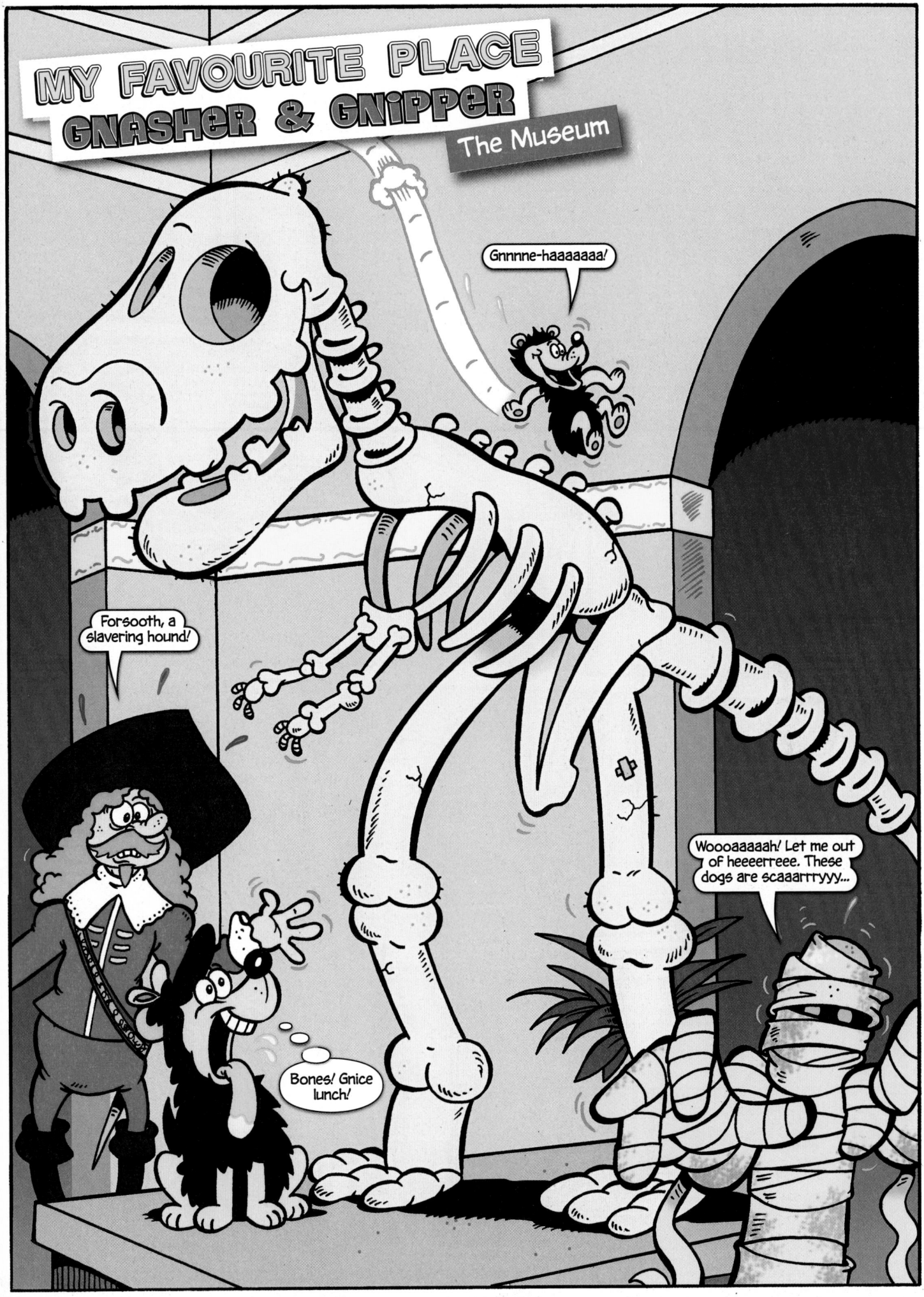
MY FAVOURITE PLACE
GNASHER & GNIPPER
The Museum
Gnnnne-haaaaaaa!
Forsooth, a slavering hound!
Bones! Gnice lunch!
Woooaaaaah! Let me out of heeeerreee. These dogs are scaaarrryyy...

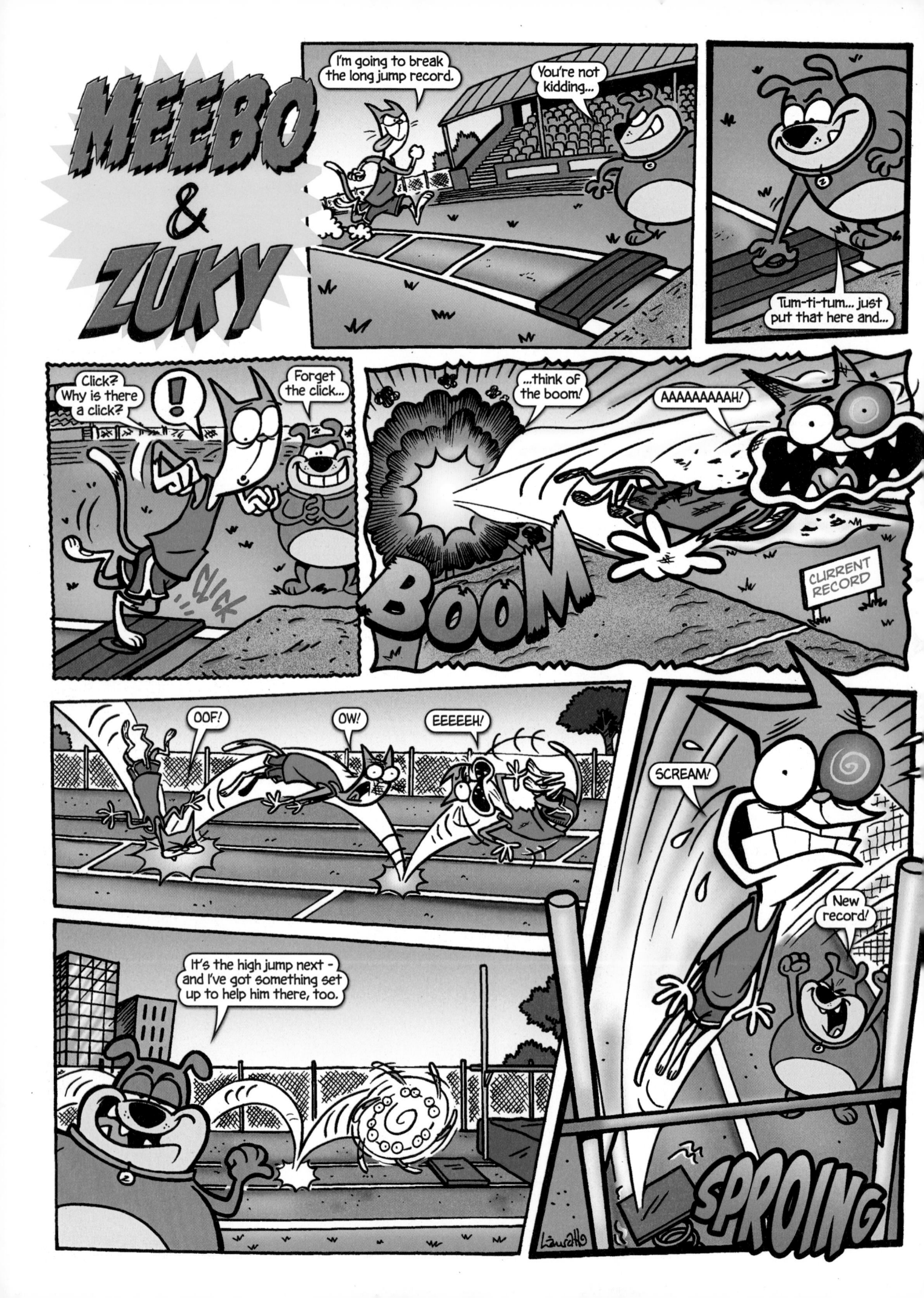
MEEBO & ZUKY
I'm going to break the long jump record.
You're not kidding...
Tum-ti-tum... just put that here and...
Click? Why is there a click?
Forget the click...
CLICK
...think of the boom!
AAAAAAAAAH!
BOOM
CURRENT RECORD
OOF!
OW!
EEEEEH!
SCREAM!
New record!
SPROING
It's the high jump next - and I've got something set up to help him there, too.

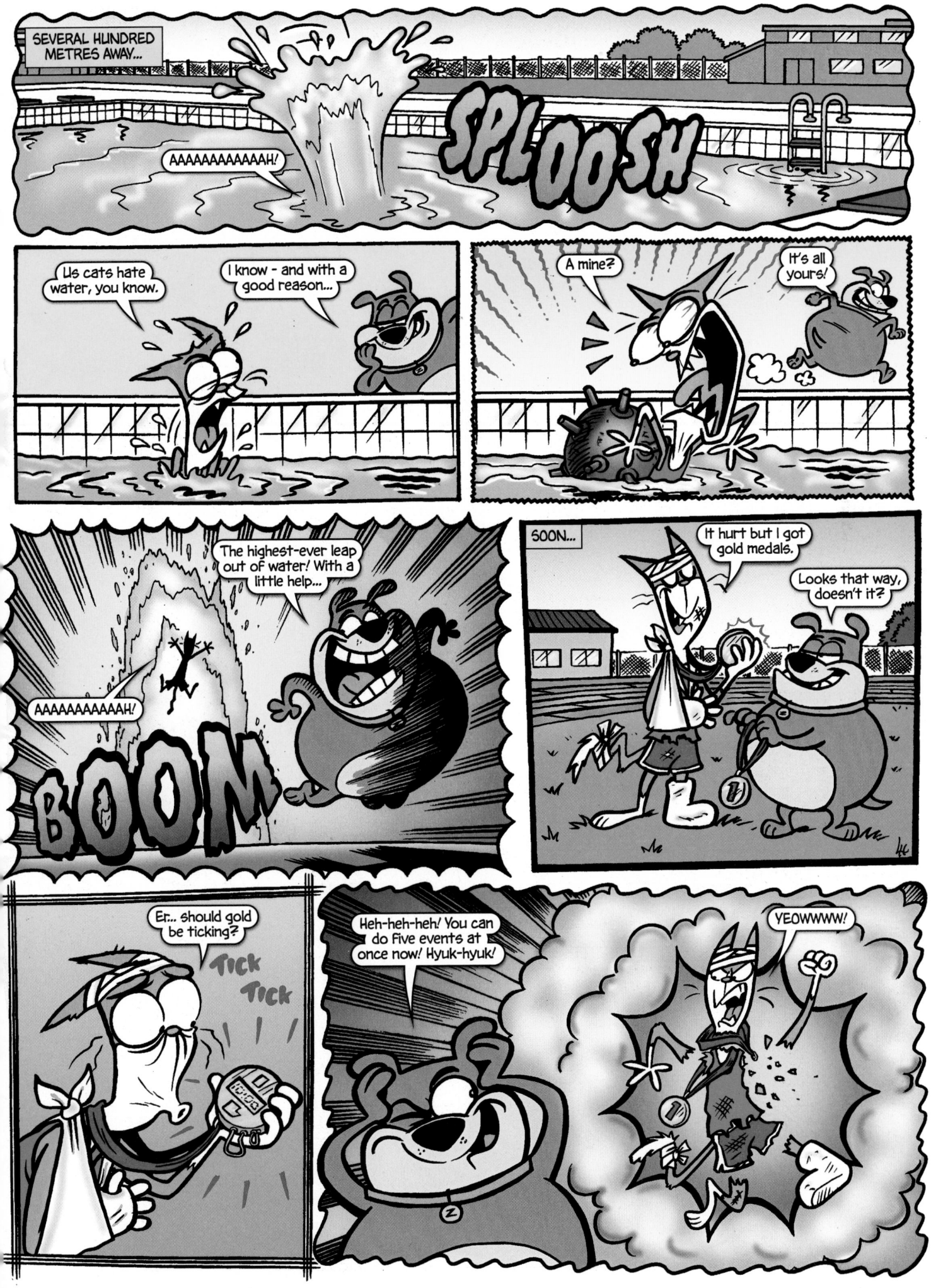
SEVERAL HUNDRED METRES AWAY...
AAAAAAAAAAAAH!
SPLOOSH
Us cats hate water, you know.
I know - and with a good reason...
A mine?
It's all yours!
The highest-ever leap out of water! With a little help...
AAAAAAAAAAAH!
BOOM
SOON...
It hurt but I got gold medals.
Looks that way, doesn't it?
Er... should gold be ticking?
TICK TICK
Heh-heh-heh! You can do Five events at once now! Hyuk-hyuk!
YEOWWWW!

KILLER
Meebo is being forced to walk the plank by the dastardly seadog, Zuky. Spot the 5 difference between these two pictures.
Finish this word search while I get rid of this mangy mutt.
You? Deal with me? Hahahaha. No mouse-muncher will ever beat the mighty Zuky.

KONUNDRUMS

Bah! That rotten, fleabag cat has blown me clean in two. Find the way through my glorious guts to bring my precious pieces back together again. Maybe then I'll have my chance at revenge against that mangy moggy.

H	Y	R	F	S	D	N	B	I
N	O	I	S	O	L	P	X	E
E	R	E	K	C	R	U	S	H
E	T	H	S	A	M	S	H	B
N	S	N	E	N	N	N	A	M
F	E	L	I	N	E	S	R	O
A	D	O	Y	O	R	A	K	B
S	E	O	N	N	R	Y	K	K
F	N	R	K	E	S	S	E	Y

SHARK
SMASH
SNEAKY
BOMB
CANNON
CRUSH
DESTROY
EXPLOSION
FELINE
FIRE

ROGER the DODGER
Cor! Should make for a cracking football match, that!
DON'T MISS THE BIG INTERNATIONAL FRIENDLY FOOTBALL MATCH — BEANOTOWN v USA XI
TICKETS
SOLD OUT!
Bah! Tickets have sold out already. Not a problem, though, for a top dodger like me!
SO-
BEANOTOWN STADIUM
Witness, readers – dodge 847. The 'act like you own the place' dodge.
VIP ENTRANCE
BUT-
And where do you think you're going?
Don't you know who I am? I'm a VIP.
Pah!
That's as may be, but if you're not on the list, you're not getting in! I've got a 'VIP' for you – a 'very impressive punt'!
BOOT!

Not to worry, readers – this dodger isn't beaten yet.
The guard won't turn away the Beanotown FC mascot!
AND-
Are you on the list?
I'm the mascot – and you need to check my ID?
Woo-hoo!
It's the mascot!
Wahey!
Well, at least I'm in the stadium. But a famous Beano star should be in with the rest of the VIPs!
I need a quiet corner to get out of this costume. No one should spot me here!
BUT-
Oh-ho-ho-ho!
Ha-ha-hah!

Who's laughing? Oh – RATS!

ROGER TRIES THE VIP SECTION AGAIN–
VIP
EN
We're the backing singers.
Fair enough. Go right in.
Aha! Good job I always carry an emergency dodge-tie!

Backing singer.
Carry on!

At last – this is where a dodger should be! With the complimentary buffet!

Time for you to come with me!
Yoiks!
Eh? What am I doing on the pitch?
You sing the national anthems, of course.

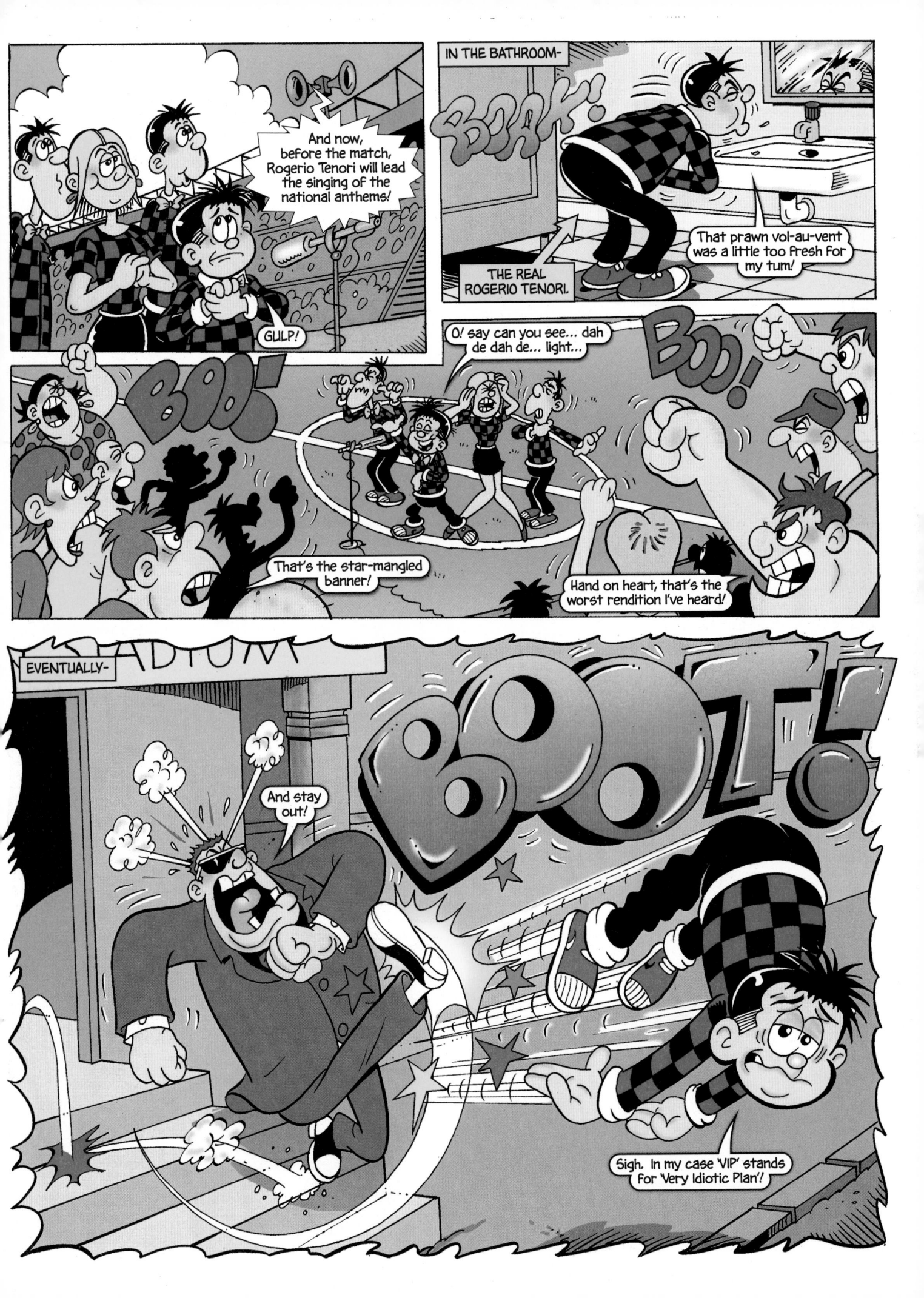
And now, before the match, Rogerio Tenori will lead the singing of the national anthems!
GULP!
IN THE BATHROOM-
BLAK!
That prawn vol-au-vent was a little too fresh for my tum!
THE REAL ROGERIO TENORI.
O! say can you see... dah de dah de... light...
BOO!
BOO!
That's the star-mangled banner!
Hand on heart, that's the worst rendition I've heard!
EVENTUALLY-
And stay out!
BOOT!
Sigh. In my case 'VIP' stands for 'Very Idiotic Plan'!

BALL BOY
HE'S FOOTBALL CRAZY!
Were you looking for this, mister?
Mr Ned! What a relief! Thank you!
The game's already kicked off – I just hope I'm not too late!
GOAL!
Oof! Sorry!
My team's already scored. Ho-ho-ho!
Ball Boy – I found Mr Ned! Oh, blast.
He can't hear me over the crowd! This should get his attention...
Sigh! Our luck's not in today.
?
! GOAL!
Superb header from Mr Ned!
DAVE EASTBURY

SOON-
BOOT!
Only thirty seconds to go... whoops! My laces have come undone...
TRIP!
Worra stroke of luck.
GOAL!
That must be the winning goal! With the last kick too!
We won the cup! We won the cup!
Championes!
And we've got Mr Ned to thank!
Ah - close enough, I suppose!
CUP WINNERS 2013!

BILLY WHIZZ
Time for my paper round.
BEANOTOWN NEWS
We've got a new delivery for you - here's the address.
Wow!
WHOOSH!
Better get going.
Beanotown flats first!
NICK BRENNAN
This lift's always out of order.
Out of order

ZIP!
WHIZZ!!
ZOOM!
THUD! THUD! THUD! THUD!
Never mind!
WHOOOOOOOSH!
Just my new delivery to go.
EEEEEEOOOOOOOW
CORNWALL
Nick, mind if I take this out? I'll have her back in a couple of minutes!
No probs, Billy!
ZOOOOOOOOOOOOM!!!
PEDALO HIRE
SPLOOOOSH!
Atlantic Ocean

South
SPLADDDSH!!!
Nice to get a change of route now and again!

SHOOOOM!
DINK
Must take care here.

LEAP!
Hello, penguins!
WELCOME TO ANTARCTICA PUT YOUR VEST ON!

I say! This is today's paper! Wonder how it got here so fast?
BRITISH ANTARCTIC SURVEY TEAM
TEA ROTA
SURVEY RESULT IT'S COLD

Not a word, readers!

Dennis and Gnasher®
AS SEEN ON CBBC!

I am going to make sure Dennis is late for school and gets into trouble.

The detour signs I've made will send him the wrong way.
SCHOOL DETOUR

I suppose we should follow the detour signs and get to school, Gnasher.
SCHOOL DETOUR
Hee-hee!

This detour is a but messy, Gnasher.
DETOUR
Gnesh!

How many roadworks must they be doing? We're going miles out of our way...
THIS WAY

...miles and MILES! You know, I'm starting to get suspicious about this.

And this is even more suspicious.
You followed the detour? This is for you, then.
PRESS HERE

Hah! I fooled you! You'll never get to school on time. You'll be late and get detention which makes me smarter than you.

Gnasher, we have thirty seconds to get me umpteen miles to school or I'm in detention FOREVER!
AWOOOOOOO!

This calls for a desperate plan.

Angel Face? It's Dennis. I'm in trouble and I need help.
I'm SO not interested. 'Bye.

She hung up!
Gnasty!

Wait a minute. Who's this?
DRRRRR!

Me again - what's in it for me if I help you?
You get out of doing any work for a while and everyone will like you more than Walter.
People like me more than Walter already but getting out of work is good.
There must be workmen in school. I'll follow the signs.
DETOUR
They must be doing a LOT of work.
Yeah... or I made a LOT of signs...
THIS WAY
... and Angel Face's signs lead straight onto Walter's signs.
THIS WAY
This really is a long detour.
A very, very long detour.
You followed the detour? This is for you, then.
Good.
PRESS HERE

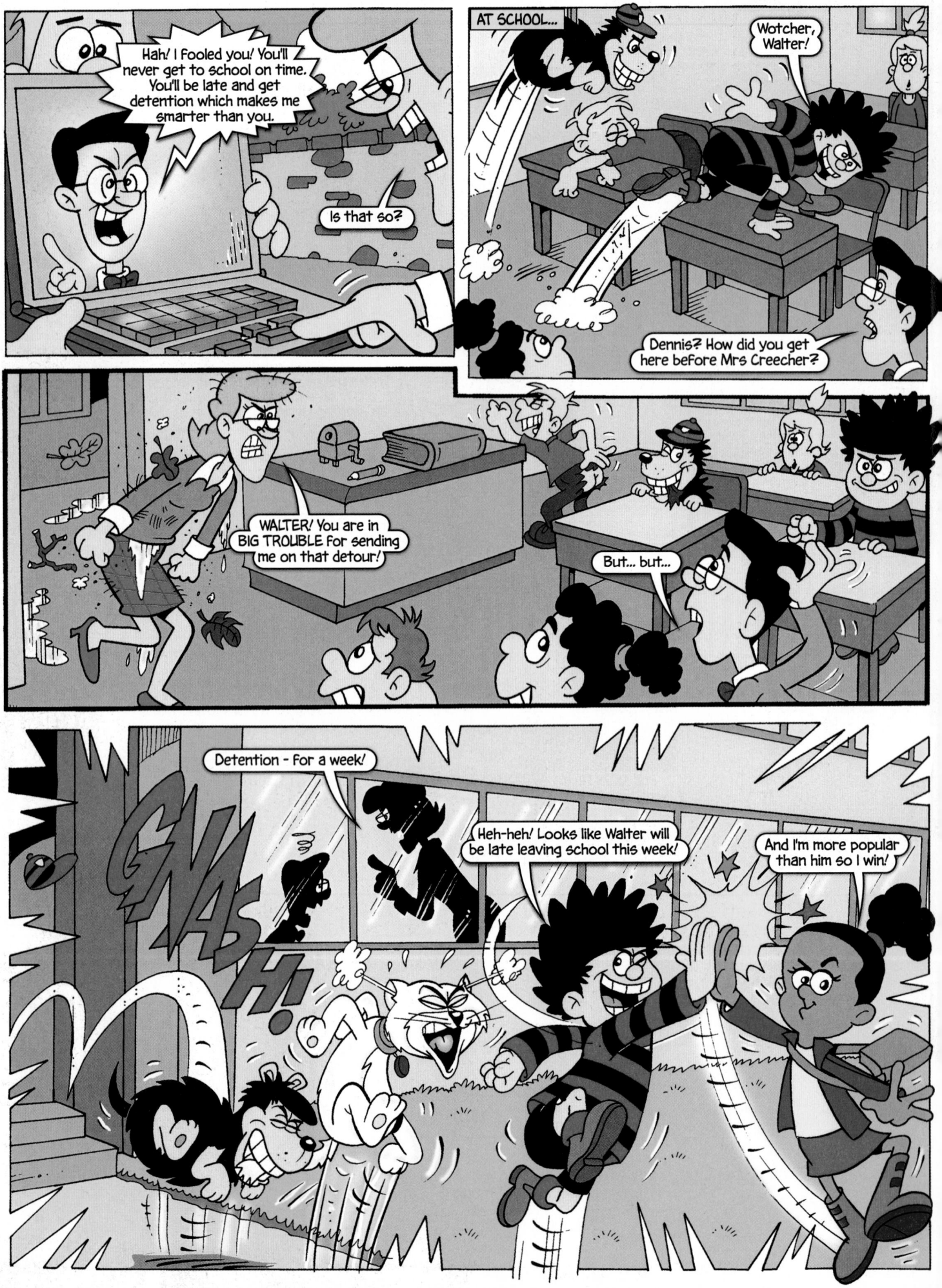
Hah! I fooled you! You'll never get to school on time. You'll be late and get detention which makes me smarter than you.
Is that so?
AT SCHOOL...
Wotcher, Walter!
Dennis? How did you get here before Mrs Creecher?
WALTER! You are in BIG TROUBLE for sending me on that detour!
But... but...
Detention - for a week!
GNASH!
Heh-heh! Looks like Walter will be late leaving school this week!
And I'm more popular than him so I win!

So many ways to MENACE!

WWW.BEANO.COM

Every Day!

Every Week!

Every Month!

Every Year!

Give gifts of giggles!
Buy a subscription for the Menace in your life or other awesome Beano stuff!

Visit www.beano.com/giftideas
or call 0800 318846
(overseas +44 1382 575580).
Lines open 8am – 9pm 7 days a week!

FART
GAS